Tinkler's Quest

A Journey Through Magical Storytelling Paintings

Judith Thompson for Stow Stories

EU Conformity Declaration
This product complies with the following safety regulations and standards to ensure consumer safety and product quality: Regulation (EU) 2023/988 of the European Parliament and of the Council on General Product Safety (GPSR): The Consumer Product Safety Improvement Act (CPSIA), Section 101. The Californian Safe drinking water and toxic enforcement act. (Proposition 65) EN71-Part 1: Mechanical and Physical Properties EN71-Part 2: Flammability EN71-Part 3 Migration of certain elements.

Published and Manufactured by Softwood Books
EU Responsible person: Maddy Glenn
Office 2, Wharfside House, Prentice Road, Stowmarket, Suffolk, IP14 1RD
www.softwoodbooks.com
hello@softwoodbooks.com

EU Rep:
Authorised Rep Compliance Ltd., Ground Floor, 71 Lower Baggot Street, Dublin, D02 P593, Ireland
www.arccompliance.com
info@arccompliance.com

Paperback ISBN: 978-1-0369-1712-8

ACKNOWLEDGEMENTS

Judith Thompson – researcher and author
Loïs Cordelia – artist extraordinaire
Margaret Aldridge – researcher
Angela Griggs – researcher
Stow Stories volunteers - research support
Steve Williams (1950-2020) – local archivist
Neil Langridge – local archivist
Tom Peer - Environmentalist
Keith Scarff, David and Margie Carter, John Walsh - nature recorders
Helen Whittaker – stained glass artist
Roy Fidler – photographer
Barbara Claridge – sister support and proofreader
Tinkler's Quest Stowmarket venues – trusting partners
Rattlesden River Valley Network – action for nature enthusiasts
Nurture Together Collective – shared vision and action for nature
Funding partners for guidance, encouragement and financial support:
Suffolk Archives, the National Heritage Lottery, Stowmarket Town
Council, Suffolk County Council (Councillor Whelham Locality budget)
Everyone everywhere who has contributed to this project – supporters
Book typesetting and e-book formatting and production support – Don Egan
Book and e-book formatting and production – Softwood Books
www.softwoodbooks.com

Pens of the Earth – Editor
Founded in 2019, Pens of the Earth is a volunteer community of creative writers, performers and artists who are using their skills to celebrate local environmentalism. Takes its ethos as 'local action wherever you are.' It features fiction, poetry, articles and illustrations from fifty-four unique contributors. It is sold to raise money for the vital work of Seagrass Restoration.
www.pensoftheearth.co.uk
Their first book *Wild Seas, Wilder Cities*

Stow Stories and Tinkler's Quest promote an ethos of caring about our environment. Together we can combat climate change through words, creativity and local action wherever we live.

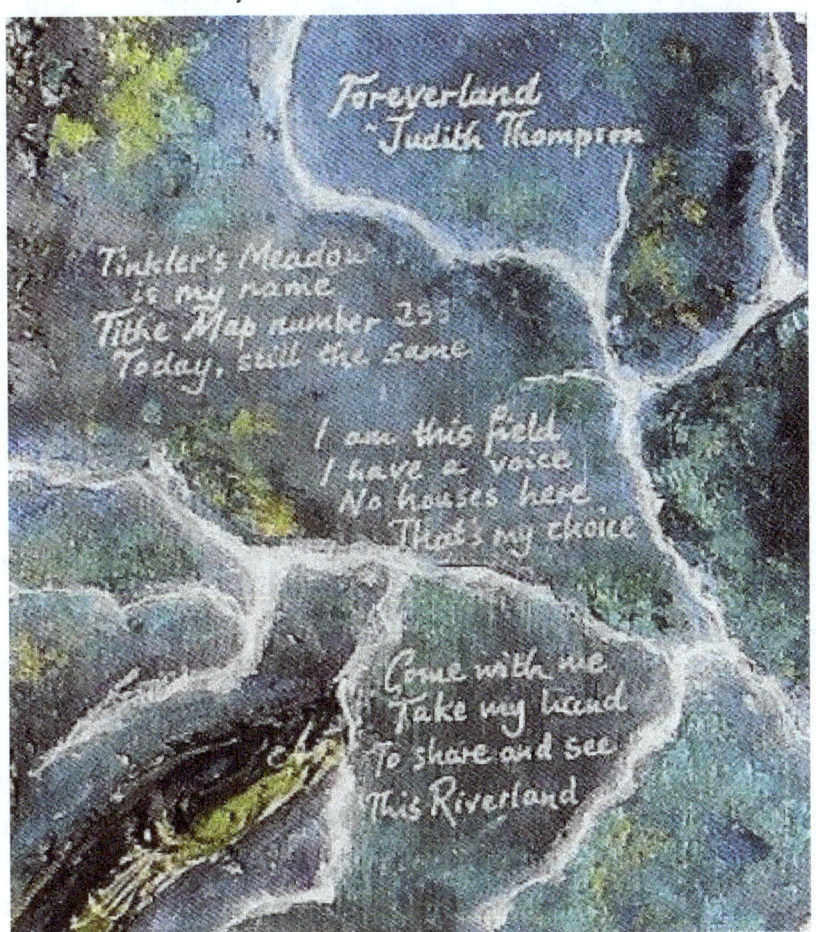

This painting is part of the Foreverland Mural in Stowmarket's library courtyard garden

You are invited to explore 'This Riverland' place, people and nature as you journey through Tinkler's Quest Storytelling Art Trail video and e-book. Loïs Cordelia's superb magical paintings promote a collective responsibility to protect and cherish the place where we live, the communities around us and the nature on our doorstep. Interpret 'This Riverland' as Stowmarket's environment and heritage.

Tinkler's Quest Art Trail video link: youtu.be/R7xYhYoDd08

Contents

PART 1

Introduction

'I firmly believe that the art of storytelling will never change. If you tell a good story, people will hang on your words.' — David Attenborough

Stow Stories to Tinkler's Quest

Stow Stories is a community engagement project to enable people to learn more about where they live, create their own responses to that place, and share their work as widely as possible. In 2018, Suffolk Archives ran a countywide programme of activities to complement the development of The Hold. One of the largest parts of this programme was Sharing Suffolk Stories. Judith Thompson successfully applied for Stow Stories to be included in this project which ran until 2022. Participants were supported to delve into archive collections to uncover unique stories about the people, places and events of their county, then celebrate and share their findings in a creative way. The Hold is now a thriving archive venue on the Ipswich waterfront.

Tinkler's Quest is the title of a collection of storytelling paintings creating the Art Trail described in this book and the online video. Stowmarket is in the heart of Mid Suffolk in England. However, the true Quest is much wider than the paintings themselves.

The journey to discover and share the history of Stowmarket and the Rattlesden river valley, to celebrate its present and protect its future, was first inspired by a campaign to prevent two speculative building proposals.

In 2018 a small field, historically named Tinkler's Meadow, which forms a vital part of the designated *River Rattlesden Special Landscape Area,* became the subject of a planning proposal for housing development.

Tinkler's Meadow abuts Danecroft land to the west. Sitting at a vital landscape pinch point between the river Rattlesden and Finborough Road, close to the town's boundary, Tinkler's Meadow provides a vital link through Rattlesden river valley, allowing wildlife and nature to thrive.

It is hugely significant to biodiversity, to local people and to the wider community.

Despite this land being outside Stow's settlement boundary, two speculative building proposals were made by developers who wanted to build houses on this land. Local campaigners collaborated with Councillors and other professionals to resist the development. As part of this ongoing resistance, the idea of Stow Stories was born.

To date (April 2025) housing development on Tinkler's Meadow has not taken place.

A great deal of research about the history and biodiversity of this and adjoining land was completed by a small team of researchers, and an amazing picture of the significance and importance of this wildlife corridor, along the Rattlesden river valley, was uncovered. Untold stories of events, people and places emerged connecting Tinkler's Meadow, Danecroft and Stowmarket, to the wider world.

To inform and inspire the local community about this important and historical aspect of the town, a grant was secured, and a series of paintings was commissioned – paintings full of images that are designed to inspire storytelling and action for nature in those who view them.

Researcher for the painting collection content

Living in Stowmarket Judith is a creative campaigner for nature who initiated the Stow Stories project. A small group of volunteers researched place, people and nature linked to Tinkler's Meadow before commissioning Loïs to create a legacy for the town. Her unique painting style perfectly interprets the research content and invites people to discover and explore Stowmarket in a new way.

Tinkler's Quest paintings promote a collective responsibility to protect and cherish the place where we live, the communities around us and the nature on our doorstep.

The Artist

Based in Scotland, UK, Loïs Cordelia is a versatile community artist, speed-painter and sculptor. From intricate scalpel papercuts to speed-painting and dramatic sculptures, her artwork spans a wide range of mediums, styles and scale, always balancing precision with free-flowing energy.

Loïs says ' I seize every opportunity to reference environmental themes in my artwork and spread awareness of the interconnectedness of biodiversity.'

Loïs's art has featured in public art trails across the UK, including many designs for Wild in Art and similar schemes. Since 2016, the combined sales of Loïs's public art pieces, handmade miniature replicas and silent auctions have raised more than £150,000 for numerous charities.

PART 2

The Paintings

The Tinkler's Quest Art Trail is a collection of storytelling paintings found at various locations around the town. Each painting is filled with images to trigger memories, spark conversation, and connect to people's emotions and experiences. Painting content reflects stories within stories.

Volunteers and artist agreed paintings would include:

– Stow Stories volunteers research – places, people, nature, historic events

– Layers of interest – landscape, biodiversity, Danecroft, industry

– Elements to represent or symbolise 'bigger' stories

– Intrigue – past, present and future connections

– Essentials - fairy-tale, engaging, magical qualities – with a sense of fun

– Aspects to foster interaction with all age groups – wide appeal

– Reference to industries and Stowmarket raw materials

– Shifts in society through time

– Nature images in Helen Whittaker's stained-glass church windows

– Something new for Stowmarket

The locations of the paintings can be discovered using the links under each painting or by using the what3words app to locate each venue by typing the listed 3 words into the app. Find out more about each venue by using the links below.

Painting titles and venue location information:
A Greener Future – Bonitas
///deeds.reflected.below
www.bonitaswholefoods.com

Round and About - John Peel Centre for Creative Arts
///sideburns.cheese.gather
www.johnpeelcentre.com

Settlement - St Peter's and St Mary's
///piper.worlds.fenced
www.achurchnearyou.com/church/2087

Home in the Universe - Stowmarket Library
///cultivation.cookbooks.parties
www.suffolklibraries.co.uk/visit/libraries/stowmarket-library

Reflect and Hope - Old Fox Yard
///amending.kipper.galleries
www.oldfoxyard.co.uk

Life Goes On -The Regal Cinema
///movie.farms.instilled
www.regalstowmarket.co.uk

Web of Lifelines - Red Gables
///brothers.skies.glue
www.redgables.org.uk

River and Land - Food Museum
///foods.rainfall.inflation
www.foodmuseum.org.uk

Pushing Boundaries - Earth Champions

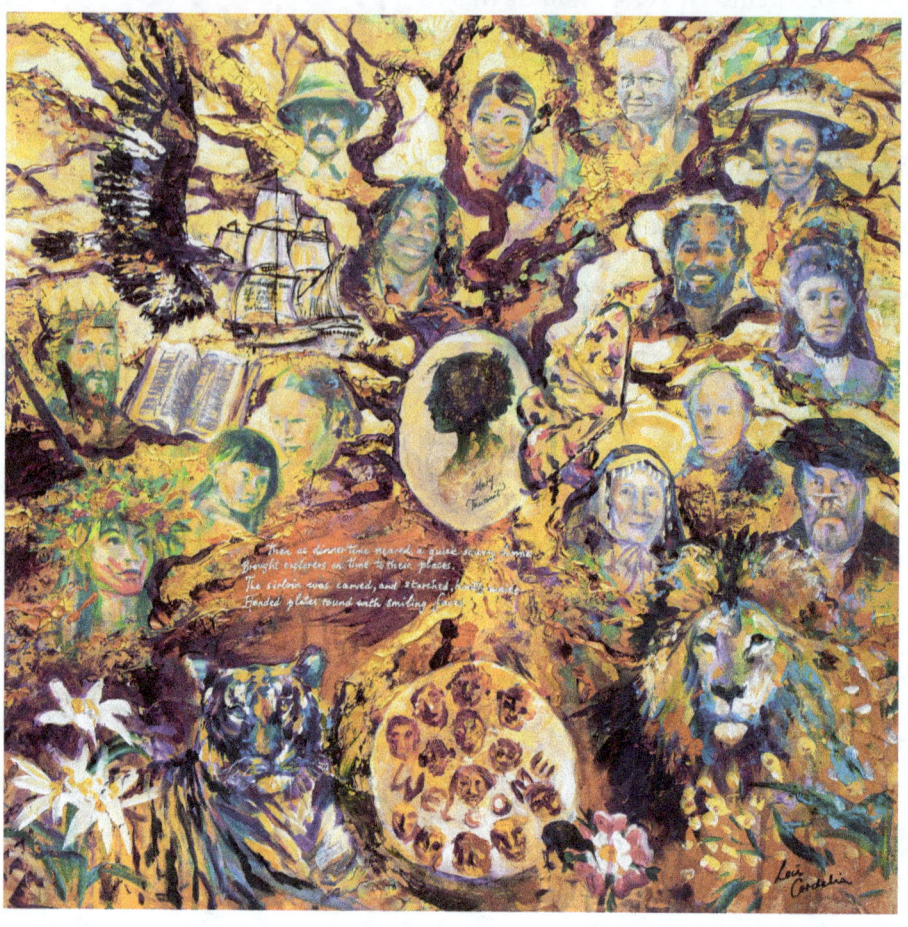

Location: *(Google maps)* Café on the Rec *(What3words)* ///stimulator.surprises.thick

Concept:

In my mind's eye I saw a tree, deep rooted with arm-like open branches holding floral emblems or symbols of nature and portraits of people linked to the countries they were born in. The people began life without fame but became well known locally, nationally or internationally. Through influences in their own lives, the choices and decisions they made, have all benefitted society. Explore and research who's who in this painting.

Inspiration:

A magnificent oak tree stands broad and tall on a Danecroft woodland track, a perfect environment for thousands of nature's species. A tree of life.

'Imagine all the people sharing all the world, you may say I'm a dreamer but I'm not the only one. I hope someday you'll join us, and the world will live as one.' — *John Lennon*

Riverline connects to shoreline, shoreline to horizon line, landline to treeline. We are all connected.

Content:

An unusual mix of characters perch in a tree of life. Each provides a snapshot of social history around the world during different time periods. They all have remarkable stories to share. This painting aims to inspire others to be earth champions through their small actions for nature.

Mary Fancourt – Danecroft Days:

Mary wrote a lot about adventures exploring local nature places and she shares a sense of fun about family life at home.

Then as dinner-time neared, a quick scurry home
Brought explorers on time to their places,
The sirloin was carved, and starched, kindly maids
Handed plates round with smiling faces

Reflection - Judith as Researcher:

'Tell me a fact, and I'll learn. Tell me a truth, and I'll believe. But tell me a story, and it will live in my heart forever.' Native American. Researchers are travellers through time and Stow Stories has been a journey of time and discovery. We have unearthed a treasure chest of connections from people, place and nature, past and present to future. What do you find most interesting about some of their stories? What could you do to give nature a helping hand?

Reflection - Loïs as Artist:

Inspired by the timeless symbol of the tree of life, this painting links Stowmarket's legacy with an array of individuals, more than half of whom are directly connected with the town and references many more people and places through the inclusion of other imagery, flora and fauna. Whose portraits would you include in your tree of life? Why would you include them?

Who's Who in the painting?

Mary St. J Fancourt (central silhouette)
1898 to 2002
Born in India, Lived in Danecroft Villa and in Aldeburgh UK.
Mary was a Land Girl in Stowmarket. She wrote 'They Dared to be Doctors' about the lives of two women named Elizabeth, the first women to qualify as Doctors. and 'The People's Earl – A Life of Lord Shaftesbury.' Lord Shaftesbury was president of the Ragged School Union, which promoted the education of poor children. He believed that children were to be treated and educated well. Lord Shaftesbury believed education was a way of freeing children from poverty. Ragged Schools gave poor children some education for the first time.

Elizabeth Garrett Anderson
1836 to 1917
Born in Whitechapel, east London
First female to qualify as a UK physician and surgeon, and the first female Mayor in England (Aldeburgh). Elizabeth's sister was Millicent Fawcett, a renowned suffragette. A modern woman 100 years ahead of her time.

Louisa Garrett Anderson
1873 to 1943
Born in Aldeburgh
CBE and daughter of Elizabeth Garrett Anderson. She had to go to Paris and teach herself French to gain her medical degree in 1870. She was a

medical pioneer – a physician and a senior surgeon who campaigned for women's rights and social reform.

Ilima-Lei Macfarlane
Born in Honolulu, Hawaii, USA 1990
Flyweight Boxer, former Bellator Women's Flyweight World Champion. Voice opposing violence against Indigenous women in the United States and Canada.

King William I (the Conqueror) and the Doomsday Book 1086
Born in Falaise, France in 1027.
King of England after the Battle of Hastings in 1066
In 1086, King William I (the Conqueror) wanted to find out about all the land in his new kingdom: who owned which property, who else lived there, how much the land was worth and therefore how much tax he could charge, so he sent official government inspectors around England to ask questions in local courts.

Adedoyin Olayiwola Adepitan (Ade)
Born in Nigeria 1973
British TV Presenter, children's author – (The Cyborg Cat). Campaigner against racism and disability discrimination. As an infant, he contracted polio, resulting in damage to his legs that left him a wheelchair user. Paralympic Games athlete, 2004 Athens. Adepitan participated in Beyond Boundaries which was a four-part documentary in which he trekked through rainforests, deserts, rivers and mountains in Nicaragua.

Charles Partridge
1872 to 1955
Born in Suffolk, lived in Stowmarket
Colonial official, anthropologist, researcher, writer who graduated from Cambridge in 1895. He knew the key to understanding Suffolk's ancient past lay in revealing the stories locked up in the county's churches. He made it his life's work to reveal them.

Dr Purnima Devi Barman

Born in Assam, India 1980

United Nations Environment Programme Earth Champion 2022. Wildlife biologist who leads the "Hargila Army," an all-female grassroots conservation movement dedicated to protecting the Greater Adjutant Stork from extinction.

Sir David Attenborough

Born in Isleworth, West London 1926

Beloved by millions around the world, Sir David Attenborough is an inspirational broadcaster, presenter and conservationist. He first worked as a producer in the early 1950s and began to present in 1954 on Zoo Quest. Even though he is in his 90s, he continues to present and narrate natural history documentaries.

Miss Constance E Andrew

1864 to 1947

Born in Stowmarket

A music teacher and the main organiser of suffrage actions in Ipswich. She founded the Ipswich branch of the more militant Women's Freedom League (WFL) in 1909.

Hamza Ahmed Yassin

Born in Sudan 1990

Home in Scotland

British wildlife cameraman, TV presenter, children's author (Let's Go for a Walk) and Strictly Come Dancing winner 2022. Diagnosed as dyslexic as a teenager. He went on to achieve a degree in Zoology with Conservation from Bangor University and a Masters in Biological Photography and Imaging from the University of Nottingham.

Baroness Bertha von Suttner

1843 to 1914

Born in Prague

The first woman to be awarded the Peace Prize who wrote one of the nineteenth century's most influential books, the anti-war novel, 'Lay Down Your Arms.' In the 1870s she became a close friend of Alfred Nobel. The Peace Prize Laureate became one of the leaders of the international peace movement, and in 1891 established the Austrian Peace Society.

Sir William Hutt, KCB, MA
1791 to 1882
(Brother-in-law to Adela Hutt Danecroft Villa Owner)
Outstanding Political career. He served as Vice-President of the Board of Trade and Paymaster-General under Lord Palmerston between 1860 and 1865 and under Lord Russell in 1865 and was sworn into the Privy Council in 1860.

Sue Williams
Steve Williams
1950 to 2020
Stowmarket
Outstanding local archivists, known fondly as Mr and Mrs Stowmarket. In their portraits they are dressed as The Lady and the Pauper. This is an image of them in the book they wrote titled, 'Alms and Legacies' a history of the Stowmarket Charities. Both are authors of many fascinating Stowmarket local history books. Steve was on the 'team' of Stow Stories researchers.

Richard Hutt
1750 to 1820
Represented by the Hillsborough. Father-in-law to Adela Hutt Danecroft Villa owner. Richard and his wife Gilly Flower had 13 children The Hillsborough was a three-decker merchant ship launched in 1782. She made six voyages to India and China as an East Indiaman for the British East India Company. Hutt joined the 'Hillsborough' as first hand in 1790, was promoted to Captain on the 19th of November 1794. The last

voyage made by the Hillsborough with Richard Hutt in command was voyage (6)1796/7 season to Madras.

John George Hart
1786 to 1861

Owner 'in part' of Danecroft Villa

Can you discover where and how he is represented on this painting? He was described to us as a man having, 'his fingers in pies.' Was he a Robin Hood character or a rogue? Do you know where his initials JGH can be found in Stowmarket?

A Greener Future

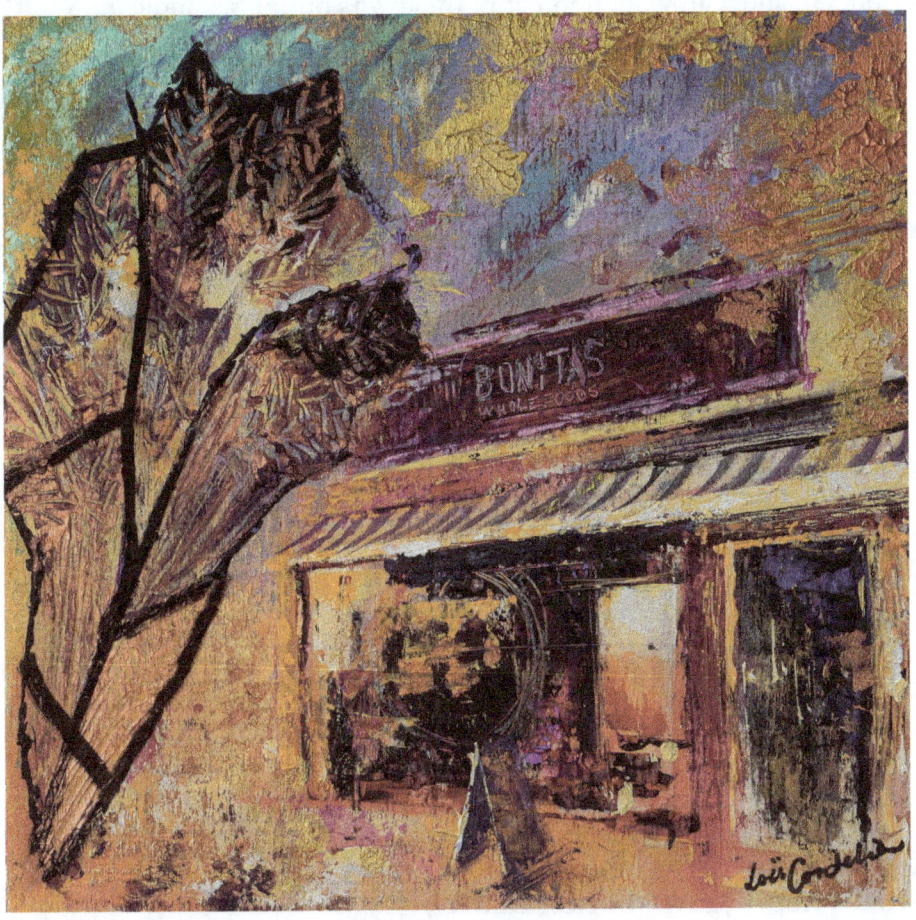

Location: Bonitas Wholefoods w3w: deeds.reflected.below

Concept:

How to capture the essence of the town's built and natural heritage and peoples' commitment to a more sustainable town in one small painting? Bonitas Wholefoods shop, both outside and inside, does just that. This painting is an invitation to look closely at built landmarks in and around Stowmarket and to encourage shopping in town.

Inspiration:

Look at the striking Bonitas building from the outside and enjoy the top-quality welcome, service and provisions inside. Stowmarket Town Council, and a growing number of the town's businesses and community groups are committed to a more sustainable and greener future, the preservation of the town's ancient character with evidence of pre- Saxon and Roman Settlement.

Content:
In this painting, vibrant golden colours capture the richness of harvest crops. Meandering patterns of blue skies represent Stowmarket's' two rivers. An inviting window display offers a warm welcome to customers to pop in to sit awhile, look around or shop.

Mary Fancourt – Danecroft Days:
Mary Fancourt wrote about her childhood memories of her life at Danecroft. Verses of her poem set Stowmarket's historic 'sense of place' in the landscape.

'Those early years living in the country were full of delights to us children.
Our greatest joy was provided by the little slow-flowing stream
which meandered between water-meadows only just below our orchards.'

Reflection - Judith as Researcher:
The free and simple pleasures we find in nature continue to offer delights to young and old. Nature's harvest provides quality ingredients for healthy food to eat and sustainable products to wear and to use in our homes.

Reflection - Loïs as Artist:
This quite simple composition connects the Bonitas Wholefoods shopfront with Helen Whittaker's beautiful stained-glass window of a wheatsheaf design in the parish church window. I reinterpreted both in a painterly style full of iridescent colours and textures to suggest the rich bounty of nature. What are your top ten nature favourites, whether to look at or to eat?

Round and About

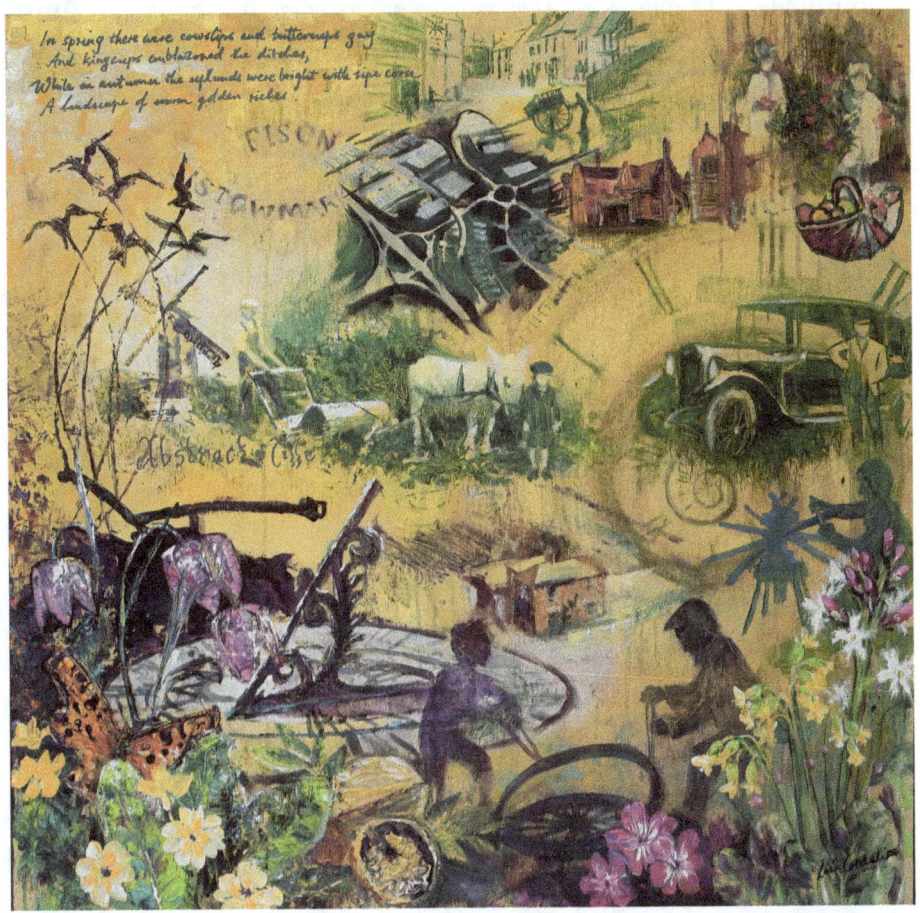

Location: The John Peel Centre for Creative Arts w3w: sideburns.cheese.gather

Concept:

In the painting, clocks, cogs, circles, wheels, hoops, and spirals interconnect; they depend on each other to function. They represent seasonal, human activity relating to the land, whether historical or a nod to Stowmarket's Gateway 14 future, where a different relationship with the land will become evident.

Inspiration:

The repetitive cycle of nature's seasons, and a Swedish botanist's clock,

(Carl Linnaeus: 'Keeping Time with Flowers') influenced this painting. Traditional seasonal activities such as permaculture, horticulture, floriculture and farming remain evident in the Rattlesden River Valley. The rich quality of the land led to Stowmarket's prosperity.

Content:

Images of tools and trade symbolise past and present industries in Stowmarket. They represent the development of machines and engineering and the advancement of technologies. Wheels and curves in sundial and a clock spiral symbolise change through time. Images include hints of distant lifestyles and iconic buildings which 'grew' out of the landscape. Human dependence on nature is constant.

Mary Fancourt – Danecroft Days:

Mary wrote about the wonder of colourful flowers emerging in spring and changes in the landscape into autumn. She finds pleasure in describing her nature observations.

In spring there were cowslips and buttercups gay,
And kingcups emblazoned the ditches,
While in Autumn the uplands were bright with ripe corn –
A landscape of warm golden riches

Reflection - Judith as Researcher:

Understanding and respecting Stowmarket's natural and built heritage has the potential to enrich us all. Expansion and growth in both industry and housing is taking place, given the town's location. If we lighten our footsteps, we could lessen negative human impact on the environment and loss of nature.

Reflection - Loïs as Artist:

Time can be viewed in a linear fashion, or in a cyclical pattern of minutes, hours, days, months, years, centuries. These patterns are echoed in the circular shape of clocks, sundials and wheels and embodied in the changing seasons of agriculture and nature. In our fragmented, digital world, what simple steps can we all take to reconnect with these timeless circles and seasons?

Settlement

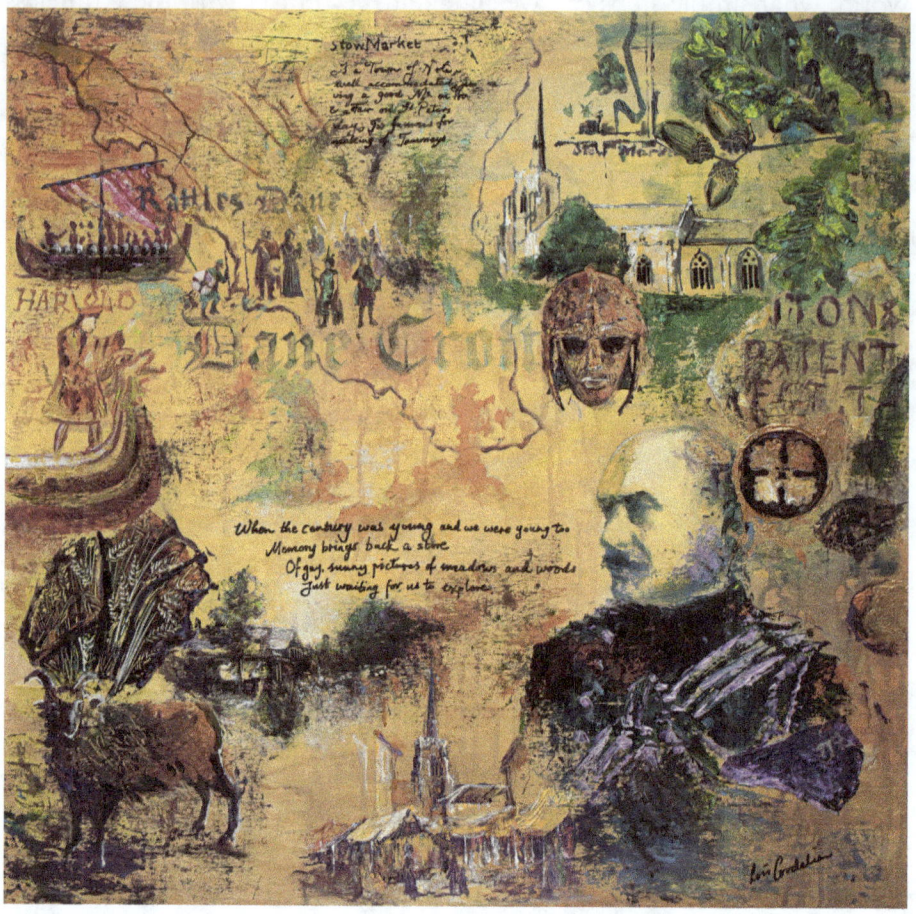

Location: St Peter's and St. Mary's Church w3w: piper.worlds.fenced

Concept:

Stowmarket is in the heart of Mid Suffolk, various routes cross north, south, east and west. This has been a travelling place for thousands of years. The two rivers and landscape of rolling hills and wooded valley meadowlands of High Suffolk give Stowmarket its unique sense of place through history.

Inspiration:

This painting is dedicated to local archivist Steve Williams (1950 -2020), who told us he had the 2000 yr history of Stowmarket in a bag. Drawn into Stow Stories through an endless stream of questions during Covid, his knowledge, sense of fun, willingness to share information, and his creative spirit, were magical. His comic verse, songwriting and storytelling frequently made us hoot with laughter.

Content:
During Covid on a balmy August evening in 2020, Steve gave an outdoor presentation of Stowmarket's 2000-year history to a small group at Danecroft. His map number 1, which showed the earliest known settlement, was of Danecroft and its river valley landscape. The very place Mary Fancourt describes in her poem. This painting perfectly captures much of the content of Steve's 2000-year history in a bag. I would have loved to have been able to share this Stow Story legacy with him.

Mary Fancourt – Danecroft Days:
Mary Fancourt wrote about her childhood memories and the joy of nature on her doorstep by the river Rattlesden when living at Danecroft Villa.

When the century was young, and we were young too,
Memory brings back a store
Of gay, sunny pictures of meadows and woods
Just waiting for us to explore

Reflection Judith as Researcher:
Everyone wants a place to call home, somewhere that matters to them. I love maps, they can be digested like a book and hidden stories unfold the more you look or read.

Reflection Loïs as Artist:
A map is a magic carpet for the mind. The land on which you stand today is steeped in history. Whether you dig up the soil to find archaeological artefacts or dig into research archives, you will find a richly layered tapestry of Stow Stories, intricately woven and interwoven with the lives of

countless settlers, dwellers and visitors. What stories about Stowmarket do you remember experiencing or being told?

Home in the Universe

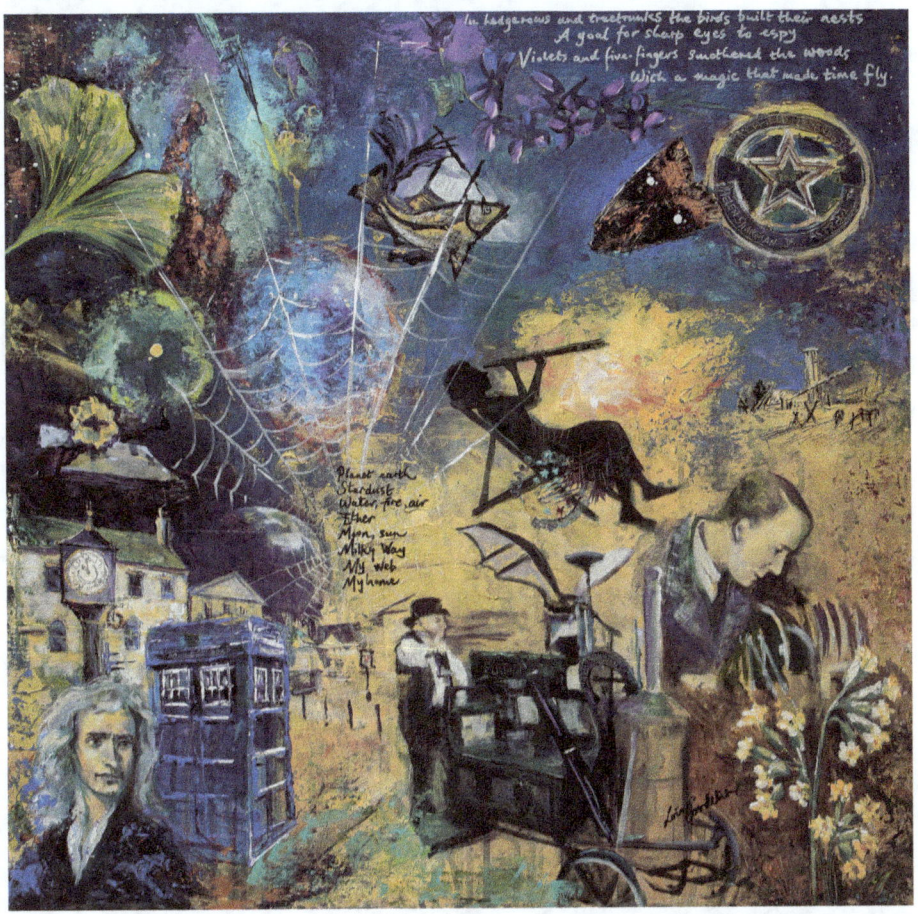

Location: Stowmarket Library w3w: cultivation.cookbooks.parties

Concept:

'Home' in this painting demonstrates that Stowmarket's infrastructure constantly changes, yet the landscape and landmarks remain the same. The two rivers and the landscape are what give Stowmarket its unique sense of place in the heart of Suffolk. For thousands of years, the town has been influenced by the people who live here, those who travel through, and those who are decision makers.

Inspiration:
Professor Brian Cox describes his home as the 'Milky Way in the Universe.' This concept expands my outlook and makes me realise we are all connected to life, on and beyond, planet earth. In my research, I discovered that Stowmarket had two famous astronomers who achieved awesome discoveries. Grace Alice Cook (1887 - 1958) who used an Astronomers Wand for meteor observation, and John Philip Prentice Manning (1903-1981) a visual meteor observer. That finding inspired this painting, as did my growing up with Doctor Who. At some point in everyone's life the expression, 'time flies,' comes true.

Content:
The built and natural landmarks in and around town connect with feelings of stability and pride. Stowmarket has a history as a town that cares for the most vulnerable in society; a town that sets sights high to achieve excellence in science, arts and literature. This painting shines a light on Stowmarket as a creative, caring town.

Mary Fancourt – Danecroft Days:
Mary had great fun when exploring in her garden and the countryside nearby. She had 'sharp eyes to espy' and gives readers an insight into her local environment.

In hedgerows and tree trunks the birds built their nests
A goal for sharp eyes to espy,
Violets and five-fingers smothered the woods
With a magic that made time fly

Reflection - Judith as Researcher:
The place Mary describes is where I live. And like her, I too, am greatly aware of the local environment in all its magnificence, which leaves me inspired every day to care about our natural world.

Reflection - Loïs as Artist:

Themes of time, space and the universe flow together placing Stowmarket on a cosmic map. What period or date of Stowmarket's story would you want to travel to in a time machine?

Stowmarket Astronomers

This is an example of how creativity feeds creativity. The verse in the painting 'Home in the Universe' led to additional research and the discovery of Grace Cook and John Manning Prentice.

Stowmarket had two famous astronomers who achieved awesome discoveries. Judith's research into these astronomers helped to inspire the painting, 'Home in the Universe.'

In creating 'Astronomers Corner,' as well as sharing some fascinating historical details, Judith wanted to demonstrate how any of the paintings could inspire further research and discoveries. 'You can pick anything that roots you to home, sense of place, creativity, biodiversity, people, the stars, to use as a starting off point for your exploration.'

Grace Alice Cook (1877 – 1958) in her meteor chair

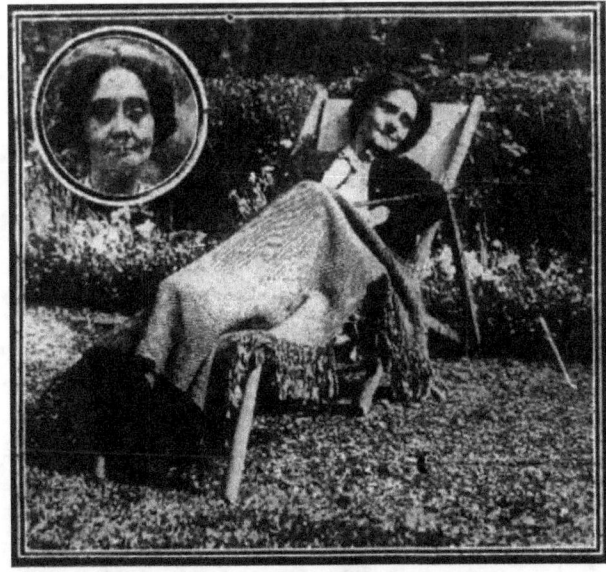

(Pictured for the Daily Mirror, 19 June 1918)

The established method of meteor observation was to use a thin, straight wand about 5ft (1.5m) in length.

Remaining mentally alert, observations were conducted from a deckchair using this wand and a stopwatch. The instant a meteor appeared, the wand was held at arm's length parallel to its path, and the stopwatch was used to record the duration of the meteor's appearance. The brightness of the meteor was estimated by comparing it with adjacent stars and planets. When the observer had all these details fixed in their mind, they were noted down. Once a night's observing was complete, the recorded paths could be transferred to a celestial globe. Taking reverse tracks along the recorded meteor paths allowed the radiant (the point in the sky where they appear to originate) to be determined.

John Philip Manning Prentice (1903 – 1981) photographed in 1934 using an aircraft navigating machine to convert celestial latitude and longitude to terrestrial azimuth and altitude.

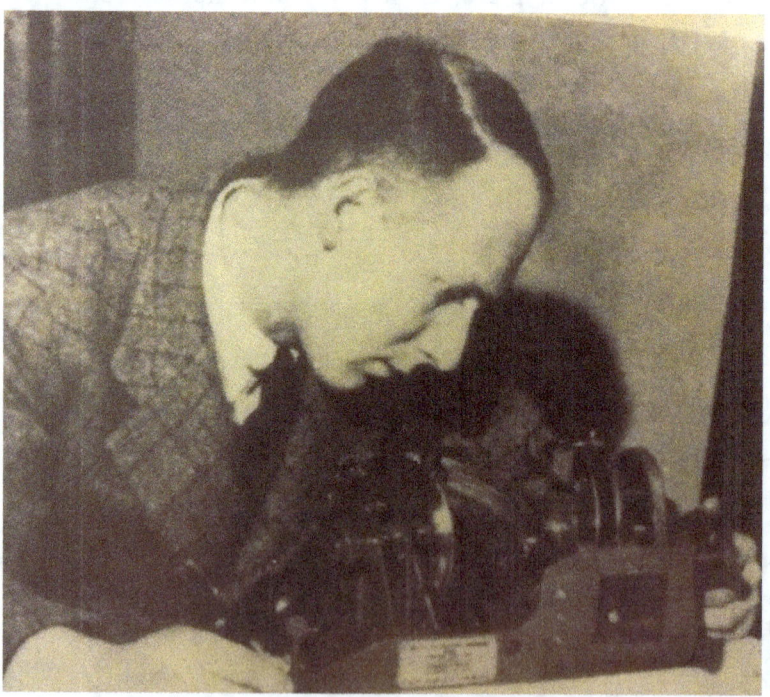

(Information and photo by permission of the Orwell Astronomical Society)

Manning was articled as a solicitor to Gudgeon, Peacock & Prentice, Stowmarket in 1921. (The firm was founded in 1821.) Eventually, Prentice became a partner in his father's firm.

During World War II, Prentice served on the 'home front' as an ARP (Air Raid Precautions) warden in his hometown of Stowmarket while continuing his legal duties. Prentice observed meteors to determine the radiant and the orbit of the particles and their parent objects within the Solar System. He was inspired to take up the observation work through contact with Alice Grace Cook (1887-1958) who lived in the same town. Prentice regarded himself primarily as a visual meteor observer and was unable or unwilling to adopt to new technology in astronomical observing that followed the War. There was, however, a period of 'crossover.' In one instance, Prentice visually observed the Giacobinid (Draconid) meteor shower of 1946 when sitting in a deckchair at the Jodrell Bank Radio Observatory, while Bernard Lovell and his scientific colleagues simultaneously observed the meteors using a radio telescope.

A Quick Guide to the History of Astronomy

In the developed world today, we live surrounded by the inescapable glow of artificial lighting. It can be hard to imagine the pristine, star-studded sky that illuminated the nights for ancient tribes and early civilizations.

Around the ancient world, Egyptian, Babylonian, Greek, Indian, Chinese, Mayan and other civilisations systematically observed and recorded the positions and motions of the stars and other objects in the night sky as the basis for measuring time and for navigation. Prehistoric monuments, such as the 5,000-year-old Stonehenge, were built to reflect the journey of the sun and moon in the sky and record the passage of the seasons. The Greeks mapped the night sky and Hipparchus (ca. 190-120BC) compiled the first star catalogue and used his knowledge of trigonometry and mathematics to predict solar eclipses.

Thomas Harriott (ca. 1560-1621) is accepted as the first person to use a refracting telescope to observe the night sky, to discover craters on the moon and spots on the sun. Although his slight involvement in the Gunpowder Plot meant his work in astronomy remains relatively unknown. A hundred years after Harriott, Isaac Newton (1642 -1726) used his theories of gravitation and celestial dynamics to confirm that the planets rotated around the sun which sat at the centre of our Solar System. Newton also invented a reflecting telescope which carries his name, and it remains one of the principal forms of optical telescopes used today.

Galileo (1564 - 1642), who lived in Pisa in Italy, found craters on the moon, the four largest satellites of Jupiter, the rings of Saturn and sunspots. His observations led him to support Copernicus's theory that the sun, rather than the earth, was at the centre of the Solar System. This belief led him directly into conflict with the Catholic Church who regarded these views as heretical. He had also observed individual stars in the Milky Way, the hazy band of light seen in the night sky. The Milky Way is the visible part of the galaxy to which the sun and earth belong. In the 1920's, the American astronomer Edwin Hubble, observed individual stars in the Andromeda Nebula and calculated their distance from Earth. These stars were so much farther away than anything else in our galaxy that Hubble concluded the Andromeda Nebula was a separate galaxy lying way beyond the Milky Way. A new, much deeper universe suddenly opened up in front of astronomers' eyes and led to the idea that the universe was expanding everywhere. Mathematics pointed the way back in time to a giant explosion that had created the universe in the most distant past - the Big Bang Theory.

Advancement into new fields of astronomy has emerged in the last hundred years as radio, infra-red and x-ray telescopes have been developed. Rocket technology has enabled the placement of telescopes into space, above the polluted, unstable and sometimes opaque atmosphere of the Earth. The Hubble telescope and, most recently, the James Webb Space Telescope, allow scientists to observe millions of distant galaxies and look back through time towards the origin of the Universe and the Big Bang.

The sky watchers of the ancient world were inspired by the mystery, size and beauty of the night skies, an inspiration shared by Grace Cook and John Philip Manning Prentice through their observations of meteors. Today's astronomers, using technology, mathematics and computers, are beginning to understand the detail of a universe that remains just as mysterious, enormous and beautiful as it has been for astronomers over thousands of years.

Reflect and Hope

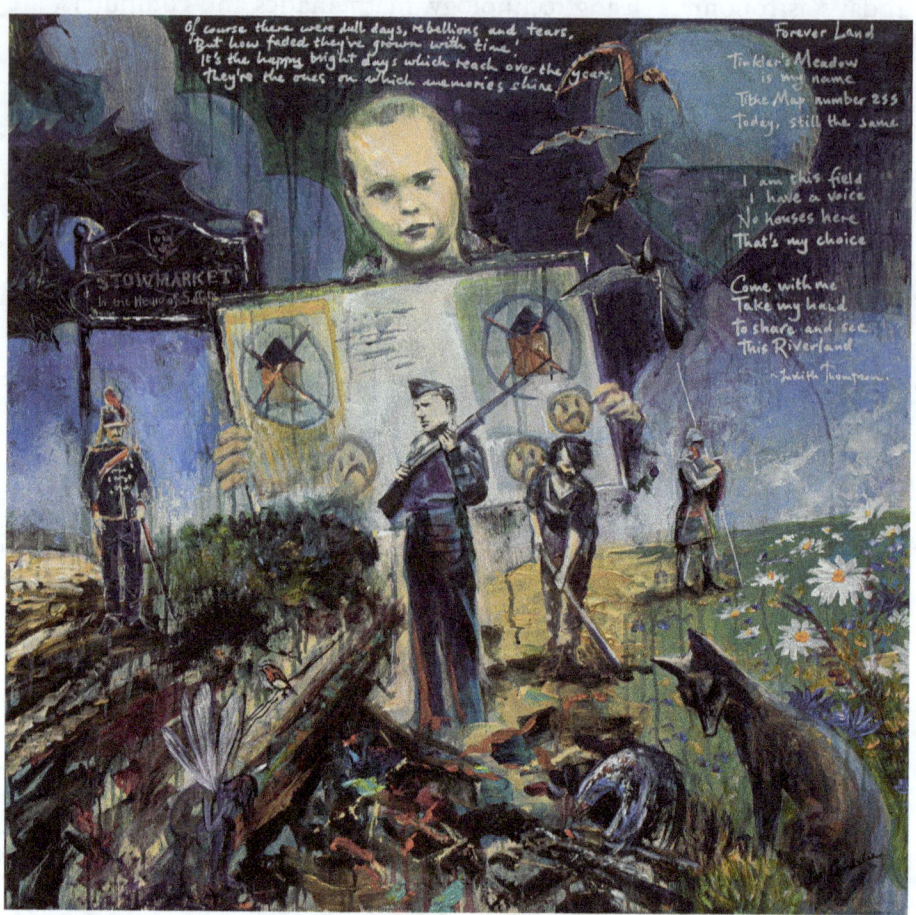

Within the painting (handwritten text):

Of course there were dull days, rebellions and tears,
But how faded they've grown with time,
It's the happy bright days which reach over the years,
They're the ones on which memories shine.

STOWMARKET
In the Heart of Suffolk

Forever Land

Tinkler's Meadow
is my name
Tithe Map number 255
Today, still the same

I am this field
I have a voice
No houses here
That's my choice

Come with me
Take my hand
to share and see
This Riverland
~ Judith Thompson.

Location: Old Fox Yard w3w: amending.kipper.galleries

Concept:

This is a painting of contrasts. When farming land and landscape features are unnecessarily harmed it is called ecocide. This small, beloved field, within a biodiversity rich corridor, became vulnerable to exploitation until community voices acted together and said 'NO.' Using your voice to speak for the vulnerable, whether it be for place, person or nature, will create a kinder, more caring, sustainable society.

Inspiration:

The natural world on our doorstep. Whatever the weather, magical encounters with nature are a daily joy and essential for my mental, and physical well-being. Creative campaigning for nature, brings hope that peaceful advocacy will be effective. My hope is strengthened knowing other individuals and organisations also care about the environment we live in and support positive action to benefit all biodiversity.

Content:

Images of land damage, hedges down, bat roost gone, surface soil scrapped then dragged into piles, saddened humans and a tiny fairy. Marching feet, figures from the past, stand fast, guard the riverside and roadside verge – they hold their nerve in the face of adversity. In this painting the Rattlesden River Valley Network and Stowmarket Eco Future Group represent Stowmarket's collective responsibility and determination to establish a greener future for this town.

Mary Fancourt – Danecroft Days:

Mary reflects on her childhood memories of play with her brother, especially their freedom to explore outdoors near to Danecroft Villa her home in Stowmarket.

Of course there were dull days, rebellions and tears,
But how faded they've grown with time!
It's the happy bright days which reach over the years,
They're the ones on which memories shine

Reflection - Judith as Researcher:

Tinkler's Meadow is the start and at the heart of Tinkler's Quest. For me, this painting resonates emotionally. It speaks of sadness and hope. Strike up a conversation, share what's on your mind. Could you share a story about a nature place you would protect?

Reflection - Loïs as Artist:

Tinkler's Meadow speaks to us through many voices. Guardians young and old from the realms of history, folklore and contemporary eco-consciousness all stand in staunch support of this virgin Riverland habitat. Will you add your voice to strengthen Tinkler's Quest to conserve this land for future generations?

Life Goes On

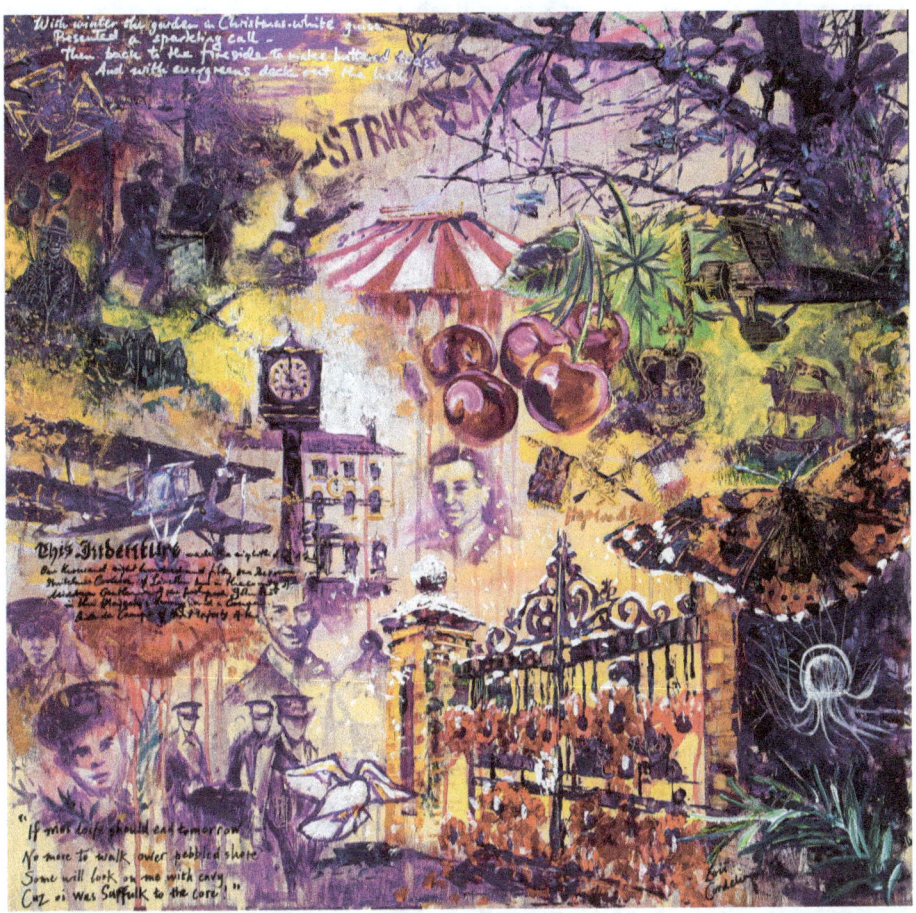

Location: The Regal Cinema w3w: movie.farms.instilled

Concept:
A patchwork of interconnecting impressions remind us of both the dark and bright sides of life. Images connect rivers of memories running through our life experiences just as water flows through the Rattlesden, Gipping and their tributaries.

Inspiration:
I drew inspiration from my family history and our research of the owners of Danecroft Villa; all have stories of love and loss. The enormity of time

and the expanse of outer space brings feelings of how insignificant humanity is. We are on earth for a flash in time. Yet during this time, we want to have 'the time of our life.'

Content:

Stowmarket in a world of disharmony, grief of past. And present day, sad, tragic events include war, explosions, disease, industrial strikes 1913 and 2023. Many elements of the painting are symbolic and representative – such as rosemary for remembrance. Heroic young people received medals but died too young. Their images contrast with symbols of celebration, love, success and memories of peaceful happy times.

Mary Fancourt – Danecroft Days:

Mary captures the warmth of her family home in winter. She expresses excitement of winter snow and the use of fresh greenery from Danecroft Villa garden as Christmas decorations.

With winter, the garden in Christmas-white guise
Presented a sparkling call
Then back to the fireside to make buttered toast
And with evergreens deck out the hall

Reflection - Judith as Researcher:

For me, this painting 'packs a punch.' It is life and death. Powerful, personal, emotional, respectful, poignant, uplifting, enriching and, cherry-picking for me is the luck of living in a peaceful place within a loving home and a kind community – that's what helps my 'life go on.' These days the programme of Stowmarket events is celebratory in nature.

Reflection - Loïs as Artist Reflection:

This painting references much sorrow and tragedy, and yet it also speaks of hope, upliftment and commemoration - sometimes in surprising ways. I chose purple and red as prevailing colours, opposite ends of the visible colour spectrum, to suggest this antithesis, balanced by green, the middle of the spectrum. How would you commemorate a loved one in a creative, life affirming way?

Web of Lifelines

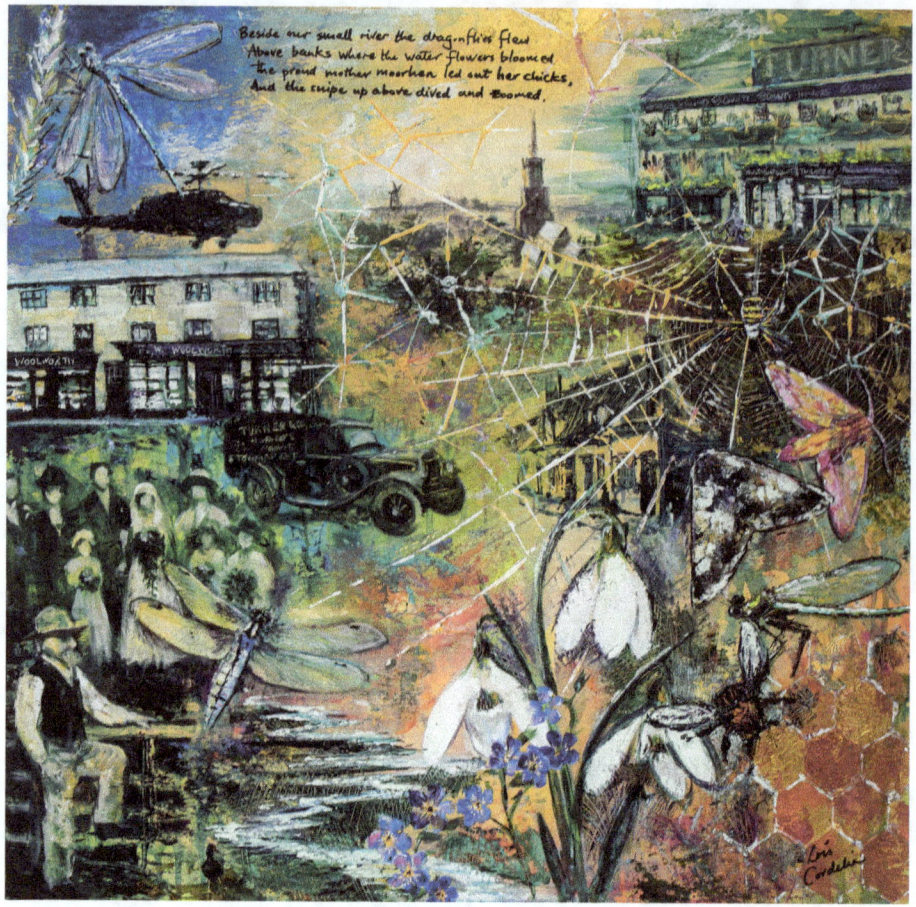

Location: Red Gables w3w: brothers.skies.glue

Concept:

To me the marketplace is like a spider in a web. Not to catch prey, but a place in the centre of the community with a multitude of lines radiating out. Production lines and communication lines criss-cross in different directions. Export and import lines as Stowmarket is the place to exchange. Through centuries Stowmarket has been known as the principal place to communicate, conduct business, and meet for pleasure. Sightline, meridian line, grid line, railway line, riverline, bloodline, B-Line, all interconnect through stories within storylines and by reading between the lines.

Inspiration:

The web inspiration threads the history of a shop called Woolworth's, an owner of Danecroft Villa and a rare mosaic of forgotten habitat untouched since the Second World War. 2000 years ago, this was a swamp, 200 years ago, it was farmed for hops and willow osiers. Read the book, 'Down the Bright Stream' (B.B.) and find storylines about the last gnomes in England who have a cosy winter home in an oak tree.

Mary Fancourt – Danecroft Days:

Mary loved the river Rattlesden landscape and the wide range of wildlife close to her home. She writes with a great fondness of nature and her family life at Danecroft Villa.

Beside our small river the dragonflies flew
Above banks where the water flowers bloomed
The proud mother moorhen led out her chicks,
And the snipe up above dived and boomed

Reflection - Judith as Researcher:

Did you know if invertebrates, insects and any animals without a backbone, were to disappear, the world's ecosystems would collapse? Did you know, a Bee-Line superhighway runs through Stowmarket? B-Lines are networks of wildflower-insect superhighways. They connect our landscapes for pollinators and for people.
Get involved, help to reconnect our fragmented landscape and make the Bee-Lines networks work more effectively. See - buglife.org.uk

Reflection - Loïs as Artist:

We are all connected: through bloodlines, food webs, transport networks, the world wide web, river networks. This emphasis on lines is reflected in the painting style, which incorporates linework and crosshatching, mostly scratched rather than painted. Do you have a storyline to share that links with themes of Stow Stories?

River and Land

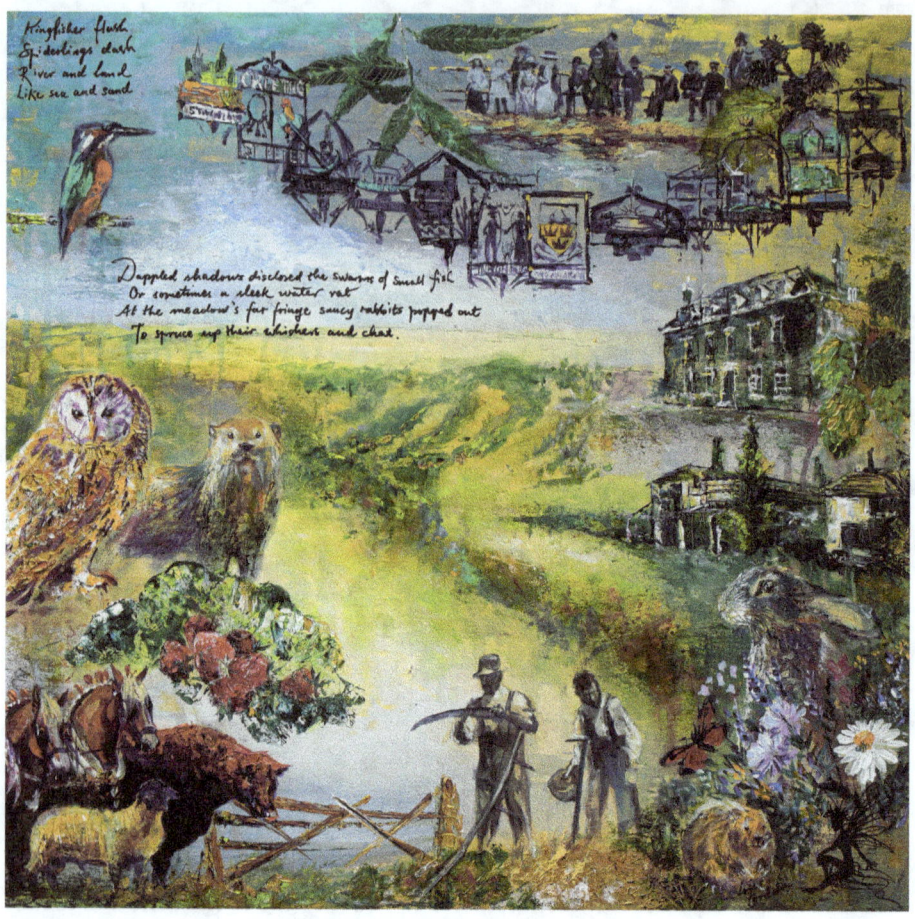

Location: Food Museum w3w: foods.rainfall.inflation

Concept:

Create a birds-eye panorama which captures the richness of the Rattlesden River Valley today as it was yesterday: an aerial tilted view which opens up a tapestry of interconnected golden fields and wooded treelines, all with farming histories. Illustrate how nature and people live in harmony in this magical countryside, west of town, where new industries began to thrive.

Inspiration:

Rattlesden River Valley is like jigsaw pieces of interconnecting parcels of land. Each piece is vital to complete the picture. The biodiversity of both rare and familiar species, which exist in river and on land, inspired this painting. Neighbouring communities are seamlessly connected in the landscape, yet each has a unique heritage. Green spaces and connecting to nature are essential for people's wellbeing.

Content:
Notice the animals of the Suffolk Trinity: then rabbits chatting with other species. Symbols of neighbouring parishes illustrate how communities share resources, and that people come together for leisure activities such as golf and swimming.

Mary Fancourt – Danecroft Days:
Mary wrote about her nature observations in the river and on land near to her Danecroft Villa home and by the river Rattlesden.

Dappled shadows disclosed the swarms of small fish
Or sometimes a sleek water rat
At the meadow's far fringe saucy rabbits popped out
To spruce up their whiskers and chat

Reflection - Judith as Researcher:
I was born near to the sea and sand, now I live next to river and land. Life itself is dependent on water. We need to care more about sea and river quality and value the landscape and settlements it supports.

Reflection - Loïs as Artist:
Imagine rising up above Stowmarket and seeing the whole landscape from an aerial viewpoint. This painting naturally evolved to become airy and bright, referencing Suffolk's famous farmyard emblems (the trinity of Suffolk Punch, Suffolk Ram and Red Poll cattle), balanced by a garland of beautiful village signs. What story elements would you include in a village sign for where you live?

Tinkler's Quest Storytelling Sprites

Each venue chose an image, important to them as a basis for these specific location inspired paintings.

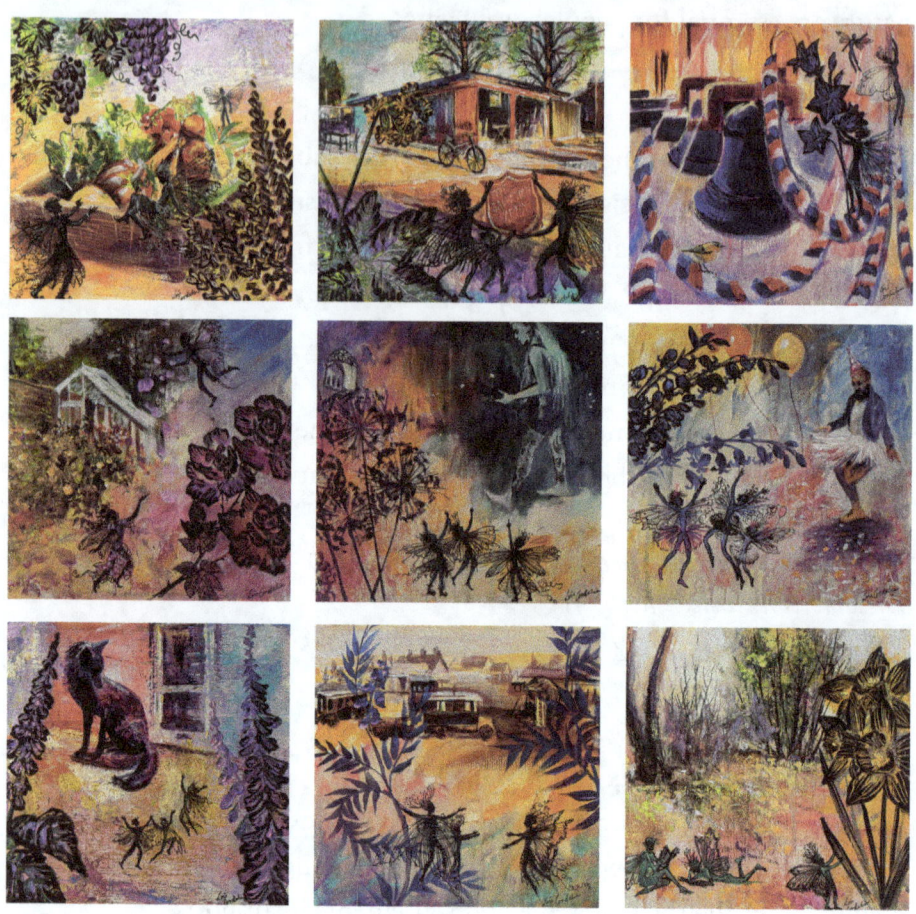

Concept:

Create something new for Stowmarket which connects each of the nine venues to their paintings and establish a contrast to the large paintings by including images that are enchanting, engaging, and have a magical quality with wide appeal.

Inspiration - Judith as Researcher:

The definition of 'Sprite' in The Collins English Dictionary grabbed my attention - 'In fairy stories and legends, a sprite is a small, magical creature which lives near water'. To a birdwatcher, sprites are goldcrests and firecrests, tiny warblers which are the smallest birds in the British Isles, and they nest in conifers next to Tinkler's Meadow. This information inspired the series.

Content:

Each small venue image includes sprites representing staff, volunteers and clients coming together to support and enjoy each venue. Sprites are helpful and kind to each other; they are magical creatures who share stories, fly, read, sing, dance, and play. One Sprite is very sad. Perhaps visitors will give them names, draw more sprites having fun or make up a story about their activities at each venue.

Discover which venue and painting are 'home' to these Sprites.

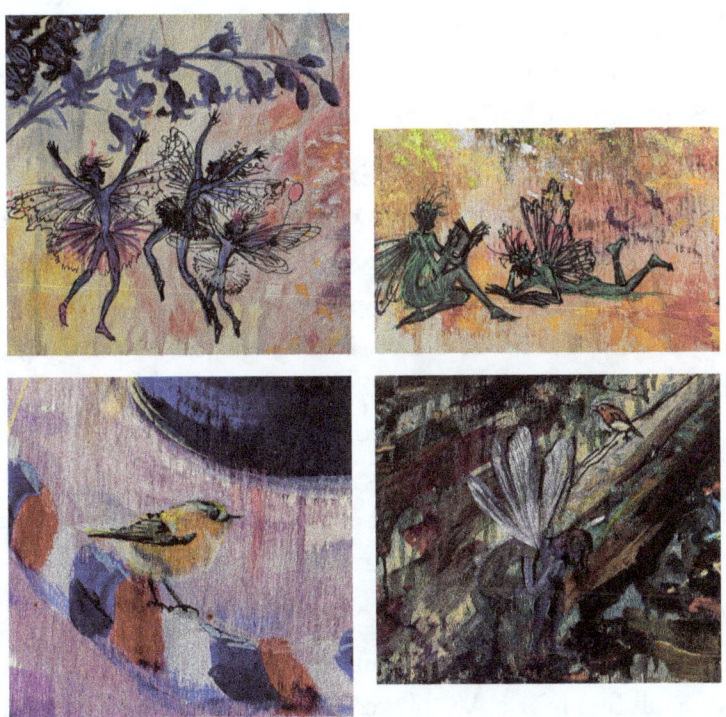

From Soil to Soil:

A letter to Tinkler's Meadow from across the ocean

Dear Tinkler's Meadow,

It's been a long while since we last spoke! Although I've been busy with my travels, I wanted to take a moment to write to you some reflections which came to me after seeing the beautiful paintings Loïs Cordelia made in your honor. I know you love to hear news from beyond your field boundaries, especially when it comes further afield from the flow downstream along the River Rat, or via the winds that blow in through your meadow from Great Finborough. Here in Echo Bay, Ontario, much like you, the lands face many ecological challenges. Pollution, development, detachment. But these problems, though similar, are not exactly the same. This is because of soil. Just like the similarities in the umbrella terms we use to describe environmental crises, each plot of land can be ignorantly clumped into one. But this simply isn't the case. Soil, earth, land – they are similar all over the globe. My travels, however, have taught me that although you can see it, touch it, smell it, and recognize earth, it is not until you learn the stories of the soil that you then understand the subtle differences that make each place unique and as individualistic as us humans. It is up to us to get to know you.

How many of us can say we know the stories of our land? You and I help to shape each other; we are codependent. Our development and growth relies on one another to the point of shaping history. So, should we not try to learn that history? Here in Canada, just as in England, there are many great efforts being made by wonderful people who are trying to help lands similar to you, be it conservation, eco-conscious farming practices, or improvements in waste management. But I've learned the strongest tool of all is when we truly become acquainted with one another. What were you before? Who else have you met? What have you helped with? What are your aspirations?

I'm currently working on a regenerative farm here in the Sylvan Valley outside of Sault Ste. Marie. We make great efforts to support one another and ensure we both get what we need. Together we grow food for our community, provide education and recreation. Just like you, the land here too wants to know of stories from beyond its boundaries – what the future holds, and what we can continue to do to ensure we both have one. And just like you, it asks for its stories to be shared. To be known. That's the key to sustainability, in all the places I have visited from Africa to the UK and here in my homeland, Canada. This Stow Stories Tinkler's Quest project is so inspiring, I truly hope that it goes beyond Tithe Map number 255 and encourages every person from every place to make the effort to get to know where it is they call home right now. For with that understanding – that ownership – we can both feel secure, and hopeful, for the future of our relationships.

Your friend,
Tom

PART 3

We are all connected

'Let us give children opportunities to fall in love with nature because you protect what you love.'

Andrea Koehle Jones: Canadian climate change journalist, children's nature education advocate and the founder of the ChariTree foundation. https://www.charitree-foundation.org/

– 'A Place That Matters'
– Landmarks
– Place Links
– A Sense of Place
– People Links
– Nature Links
– Foreverland
– We are all connected. Web of Life – Food Web

'A Place That Matters' Judith Thompson

On 16 October 2019, at a Stowmarket Town full council meeting, I Invited individuals (Councillors and Town Council Officers) to participate in the Stow Stories Project. All joined in an activity called Place Consequences.

Everyone took a few minutes to: *'conjure up a specific and favourite place, somewhere real, outdoors, somewhere in the landscape of Stowmarket. In your mind take a stroll, wander about, or just sit quietly and observe your surroundings. A place you know well. Use your senses to bring this place to life in your memory – as if you were really there.'*

On behalf of Stowmarket Town Council, I constructed a narrative by combining individual responses which reflect the essence of Stowmarket as a place that matters in the past, present and into a greener future.

This extract from Alan Gussow's book inspired this activity: *A Sense of Place: The Artist and the American Land,* published in 1972.

'There is a great deal of talk these days about saving the environment. We must, for the environment sustains our bodies.

'A place is a piece of the whole environment that has been claimed by feelings. Viewed simply as a life-support system, the earth is an environment. Viewed as a resource that sustains our humanity, the earth is a collection of places. We never speak, for example, of an environment we have known it is always places we have known – and recall. We are homesick for places, we are reminded of places, it is the sounds and smells and sights of places which haunt us and against which we often measure our present.'

Alan Gussow was an artist, writer and conservationist born on May 8, 1931, in New York City. He died in 1997 aged 65. He was a landscape painter who combined close-up naturalistic observation with an abstract style.

His book *A Sense of Place: The Artist and the American Land*, couples works by American landscape artists, spanning four centuries, with excerpts from their own writing. While speaking about his conservation efforts with New York Times critic Grace Glueck in 1972, Gussow argued that there should be an artist-in-residence program in America's national parks, 'just as there are poets and writers in residence at universities.' Soon afterwards, he convinced the National Park Service to start such a program, and took the first turn, at the Cape Cod National Seashore in 1968. 'My job was to be inspired by the location,' he recalled, 'and create paintings that would reflect experience.' He was possessed by the idea that 'once an artist puts a value on a place, it helps to preserve it,' Gussow.

Stowmarket - A Place That Matters

Undulating land, greens, blues and browns, washed in bright sunlight; this well-trodden meandering mud path. Groups of people walking, children playing, smiling. In a blue sky with few clouds' butterflies and other insect's fly. Walk from the entrance up through the wooded path into open space. Follow the duckboard to a flooded, broken river-span, now repaired.

Down the end of a nearby road there is a willow-tree place with young saplings and over-mature trees in various stages of growth and decay.

Greenery surrounds you; peacefulness within a town. Woodland, wildlife, bark textures, flowers, children, birds. Community.

Verdant Spring and the place is full of bright yellow daffodils and birdsong; a natural beauty.

Early summer: buzzing, green warmth, soft weather to easily doze in.

Autumn inside the wood: log piles, birdfeeders, natural seats, and various rooms, colours of fire, wet moist smells of earth; quiet is falling.

Winter and cold. Frost on the ground is beautiful and still.

The past is similar, beyond the change of seasons, which is what makes it special. Open the garden gate, step into the field, past farm animals and the orchard. Walk down the road, take the short cut, turn right, along the lane through long grass. Go by the camping land, the Regal, and buildings on the high street, across the rec, on through the town centre to the market stalls, turn right just before the corner, turn left at the top of the road. After the church left again before the Pickerel Bridge. With the river on your right, up the driveway and through the bamboo screen – home.

Today, as yesterday, the field remains a refuge under threat, yet peaceful and full of memories. Now it is overgrown and unwelcoming, no paths. But imagine a meadow, a beautiful open space with many trees. In times gone by monks and farm workers created an active and vibrant place, a coaching inn and stables, the chapel, a wind pump, and now a museum.

Sunday walks, no work, few chores. I sense a tranquillity when I am there and an enjoyment of the unrestrained growth and decay of plants and trees. I love the perception of stillness and of stepping into that empty space just for me. Emotion in a community space. I feel a fondness, a moving of something special in the town; a slice of serenity. All is good and better than the past. I am warm, pleased to be here in familiar landscape, calm, at one with the countryside and the engineering skills of the past. Nature and heritage.

Feel the air and remember the fairground, the circus, agriculture and architecture. I came to feel this peaceful place, to walk and run in open space, catch the train to London, or search the local history. I like the leaves and all those wonderful feelings they rouse in me. Play location; peace from disarray. Nature. I like it – simply that. And yet, much more. New technology awake and lively. The place in some way has not changed but the people have. Think, a community meeting place, more like a home, a haven, a piece of me I have only just discovered. Think, the place itself is yet to change, I am happy to be a part of the process and privileged to still have that chance.

Author - Judith Thompson
Creative Campaigner for nature

Stowmarket Town Council is supported by community groups and businesses to address the climate and biodiversity crisis.

Research shows that people who are more connected with nature are usually happier in life and more likely to report feeling their lives are worthwhile. Nature can generate many positive emotions, such as calmness, joy, and creativity and can facilitate concentration. Our relationship with nature – how much we notice, think about and appreciate our natural surroundings – is critical in supporting good mental health and preventing distress.

Walks and Wanders

Stowmarket Leisure Centre wellbeing walk with Stowmarket Dementia Action Alliance

A magical wellbeing-walk organised by Stowmarket Leisure Centre and Stowmarket Dementia Action Alliance was arranged and the group visited the land at Danecroft Cottage. These walks were dementia friendly but open to all. In this walk video, the gang visit Danecroft Cottage on the edge of Stowmarket - a nine-acre private woodland which is managed for biodiversity and wildlife. Judith Thompson hosts the group, and cardiac rehab trainer, Bob Halls, leads the walk and exercises. See video here.
https://www.youtube.com/@Walksandwanders

Landmarks a Stowmarket Storytelling Painting

JAM invited Loïs to promote the Stow Stories legacy by creating a 'Stowmarket Landmarks' painting. Loïs was commissioned to paint live during a Red Gables event to celebrate the Queen's Platinum Jubilee, to respond artistically to visitor's suggestion about their favourite landmarks' in and around Stowmarket. Funding for this was secured via the Nurture Together collective. The Stowmarket Landmarks' painting would later go on tour at nine venues across the town to raise interest in the forthcoming art trail launch titled Tinkler's Quest.

(*JAM Judith, Angela and Maggie – Stow Stories volunteer researchers)

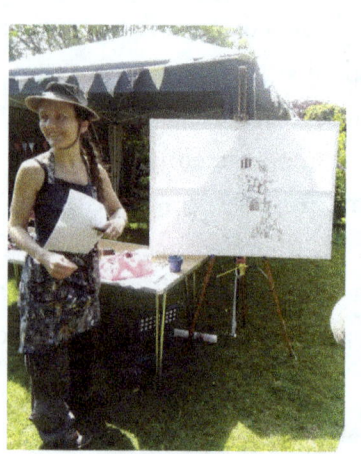 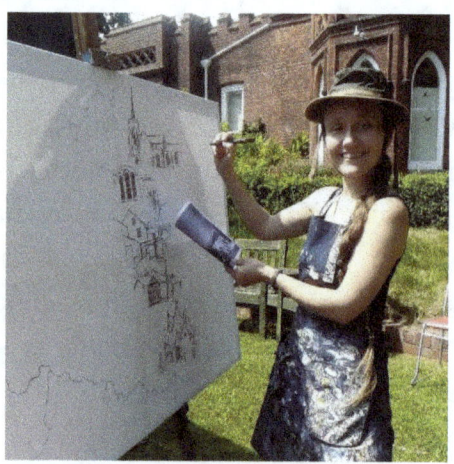

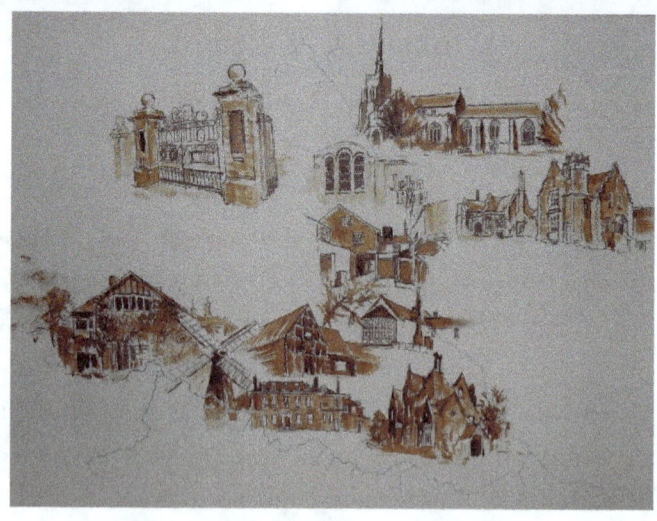

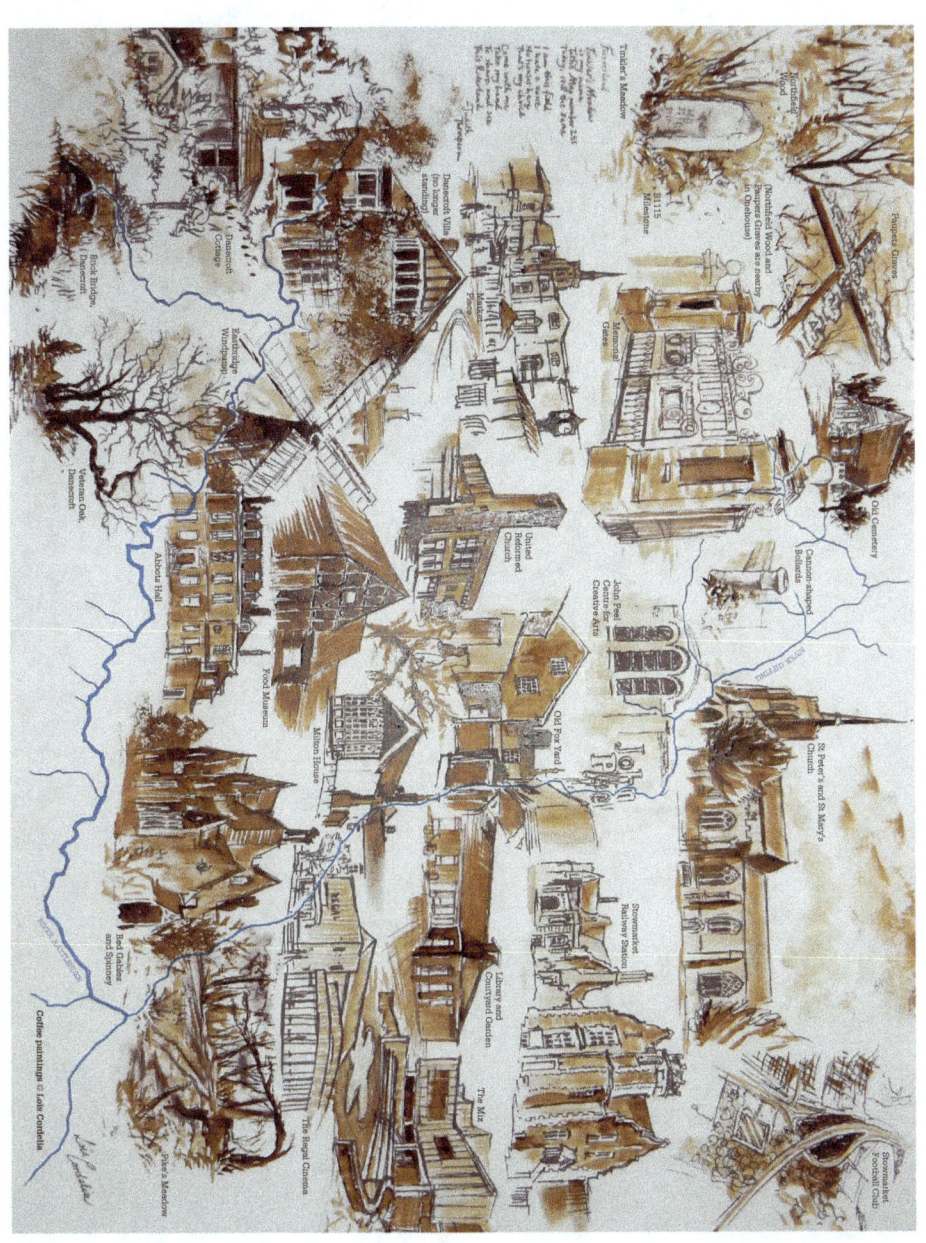

Coffee paintings © Loki Cordelia

STOWMARKET

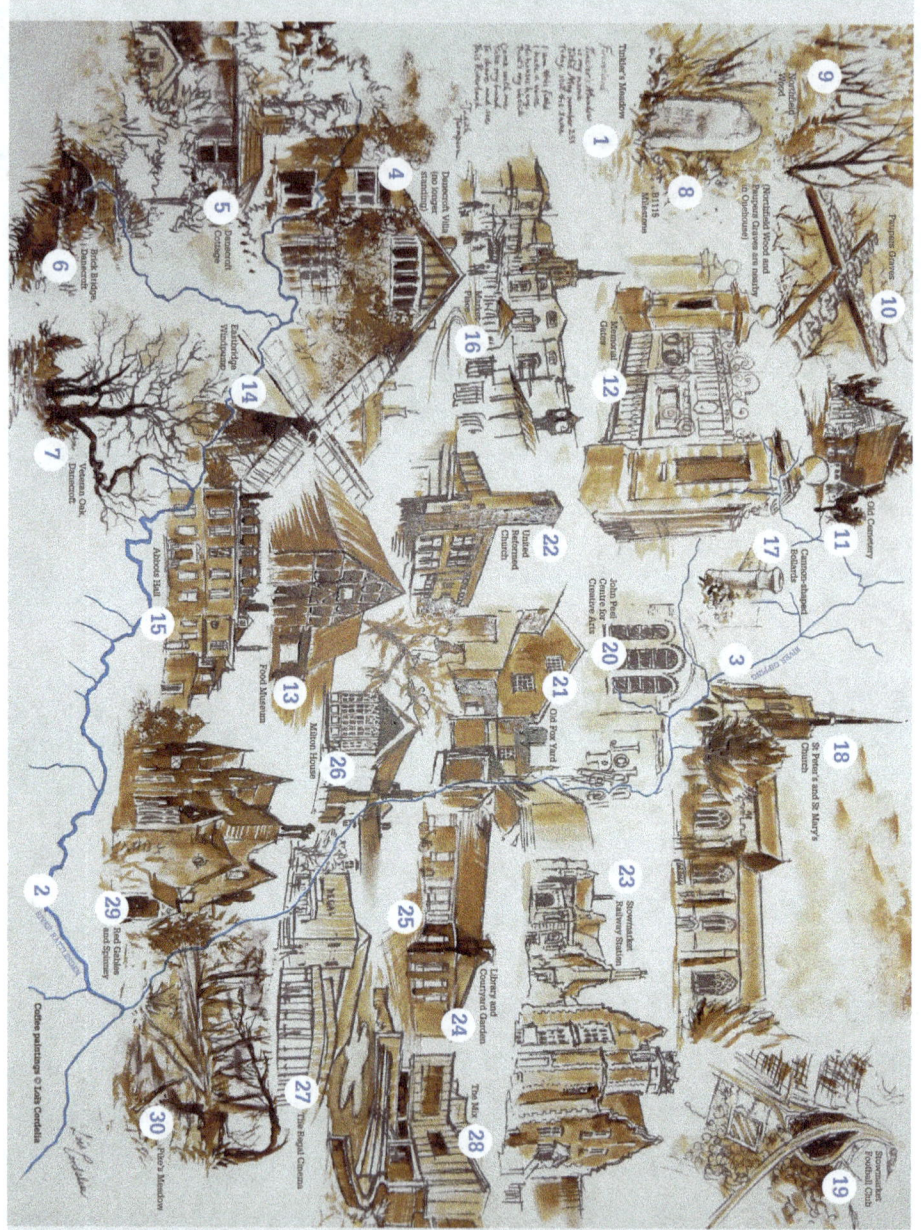

LANDMARKS

Landmarks Key - Stowmarket Storytelling Painting

1 - Tinkler's Meadow - Nestled in the Rattlesden River Valley, west of Stowmarket (IP14 1PY), within a biodiversity-rich green river corridor. It was the target of two speculative building applications in 2018 / 2019. Not yet saved for the community of Stowmarket.

2 - River Rattlesden - Historically, the River Ure (the Orwell). Stowmarket to Ipswich main river.

3 - River Gipping - There is evidence of its use for navigation in the 13th and 4th centuries. Following a new bill introduced into Parliament, navigation finally became operational in 1793.

4 - Danecroft Villa (no longer standing) - Once a picturesque home and nursery garden with land including Danecroft Cottage and Tinkler's Meadow. The starting point of Stow Stories research with a fascinating past connecting places, people and nature in Stowmarket and around the world.

5 - Danecroft Cottage - Situated down an historic woodland track named Gylleslane in the 1600's and nestled within a quiet, hidden woodland **place where rare and diverse wildlife species thrive.**

6 – Danecroft Brick Bridge - This bridge connects the north to the south side of the River Rattlesden. A place to meet, play pooh-sticks and wander onwards to five-finger Wood.

7 – Danecroft Veteran Oak – A veteran tree on the woodland track through Danecroft land.

8 - B1115 Milestone – An ancient monument, on B1115 the east to west turnpike road to Bury.

9 - Northfield Wood – Onehouse. This ancient woodland west and north of Stowmarket is a vital wildlife place connecting parcels of land along the Rattlesden River Valley from Pikes Meadow westwards into open countryside.

10 - Paupers Graves - A large metal cross commemorates graves of the poorest in society. Graves were neglected for over 200 years, until Onehouse parish council purchased the site in 2000 and now maintain it for the benefit of local communities. A quiet reflective space.

11 - Old Cemetery - An historic place now managed for nature. A commemorative plaque dedicated to those who lost their lives in the Gun Cotton Explosion is on the central roundabout.

12 - Memorial Gates - At the Finborough Road entrance, mark the dedication service in 1920.

13 - Food Museum - Offers something for everyone, within 75 acres of Suffolk countryside there are 40,000 objects and 17 buildings to explore.

14 - Eastbridge Windpump - Restored to working order in 2021, standing on the edge of the Rattlesden River Sculpture trail in the Food Museum grounds.

15 - Abbots Hall - A fine 18th century house (and adjacent walled garden) within the Food Museum site refurbished to provide nine exhibition rooms.

16 - Market Place - Stowmarket was granted a Market Charter in 1347 by Edward III (13 November 1312 – 21 June 1377), also known as Edward of Windsor before his accession, was King of England from January 1327 until his death.

17 - Cannon-shaped Bollards - They mark the entrance to the earlier Suffolk Iron Works.

18 - St Peter's and St Mary's Church - A beautiful Grade l listed building in the centre of town.

19 - Stowmarket Football Club - Founded in 1883, originally at the Cricket Meadow.(Asda land)

20 - John Peel Centre for Creative Arts - This thriving venue was a rural corn hall, built in 1835.

21 - Old Fox Yard - Originally a 16th century coaching inn, a collection of niche businesses now operate from here.

22 - United Reformed Church - A Gothic style meeting House in 1719, rebuilt in 1861, bombed in 1941 during WW2 and rebuilt in 1955.

23 - Stowmarket Railway Station - Brick built in 1846 in Jacobean style, it is Grade 11 listed building. (A building is listed when it is of special architectural or historic interest considered to be of national importance and therefore worth protecting).

24 - Library – Stowmarket had a flourishing book club since 1796, a literary service from 1873 and the current library was built in 1981.

25 - Courtyard Garden at the library - A vibrant community garden transformed with a sustainability as its theme in 2021. Storytelling murals depict the history of Stowmarket – place, people and nature and Loïs Cordelia's Foreverland Mural is displayed here.

26 - Milton House - A 16th century vicarage, now housing the town council offices. The Mulberry tree is believed to be an offshoot of a tree planted by poet John Milton (1608-1674).

27 - Regal Cinema - Opened in 1936 as a 566-seat cinema. Renovated in 2021 to offer three screens and the 1936 café.

28 - The Mix - A Suffolk-based youth work charity with inspirational facilities and services.

29 - Red Gables and Spinney - A Wellbeing Hub for the whole community. Volunteers maintain its enchanting spinney and gardens.

30 - Pike's Meadow – near the River Rattlesden and Gipping confluence. A green space, river walk and children's play area open to the public. Historically the formal gardens of Red Gables.

Place Links:

The researchers discovered that Danecroft owners, their families or occupiers had connections for example, in Westmorland, Gateshead, Newcastle, the Isle of Wight, Austria, North and South of England, Australia, New Zealand, India, Kew Gardens, the Royal Hospital Chelsea, Dartmouth, Stowmarket itself and the surrounding area.

The painting River and Land at the Food Museum depicts the Suffolk Trinity – a Suffolk Punch horse, a Redpoll bull and a Suffolk ram and a necklace of village signs (two small parts of this paintings below). In this painting these images symbolize communities connected through time by river and land. Stowmarket's Old Bathing Place was on the river Rattlesden near to Combs Ford. Swimmers took the plunge while onlookers dressed in their Sunday best cheered them on.

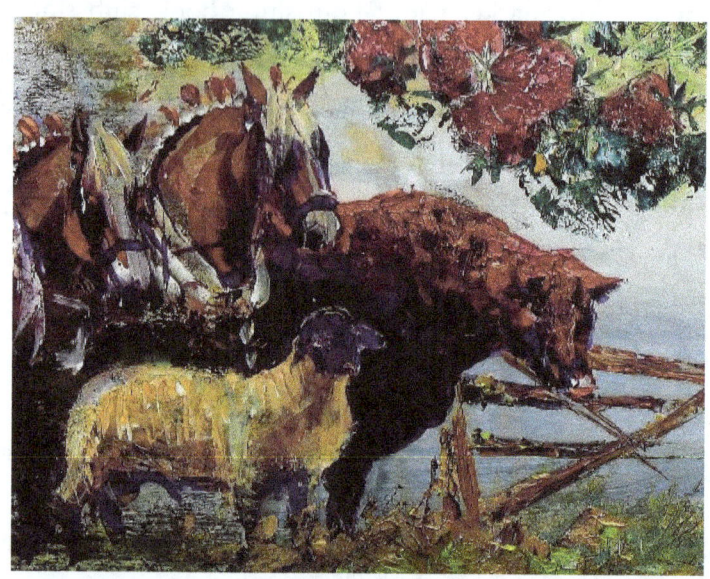

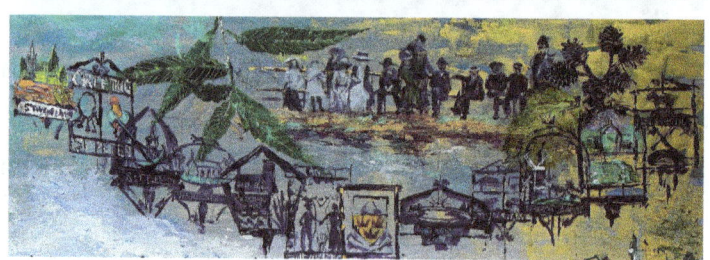

Danecroft Villa

This was a picturesque residence in a prominent position on Finborough Road about a mile from Stowmarket town centre. The Villa was demolished around 1960, and Beaumont Way and West View properties were built on the villa land. Mary's father was Brigadier General St. J. F. M. Fancourt C.B.

Mary Fancourt's parents bought the villa in 1906, and the family moved to London in 1918 after her father died. The villa was sold for £1,500.

In her journal Mary describes her home when it sold:

'the house, with eight or 9 bedrooms, and property of twelve acres where there were water meadows along the valley bottom and arable land on the higher ground on either side.'

Describing Danecroft in more detail Mary wrote:

'The house had only one storey above the first floor. It had not been built for what the Wiggins uncles would have called 'A gentleman's residence'. Father added more rooms here and there as needed. It was certainly rambling, with steps up and down into rooms and passages at varying levels. But, strangely enough, the whole effect was very pleasing. Cooking was done on a big coal range, with a spit for roasting. There was tap water in the house, but it had to be pumped up by hand. The gardener did a twenty-minute stint morning and evening at the pump. There was no electricity or gas. Rather beautiful silver lamps, with big white silk shades, were brought in when it grew dark. Upstairs, we had small lamps in brackets and candles.'

'Our garden too was rambling, and there were three orchards. When father was smitten with a creative urge he would incorporate bits of orchard into the garden and make another small lawn or shrubbery. It was all very haphazard, but he seemed to have a certain flair for landscaping and the whole turned out very attractive. He knew nothing about practical gardening, neither did mother, nor, in fact did the gardener, Walter Turner, a countryman with an adjacent cottage who came to work for us. Mother quickly realised that if she was to get the kind of flower garden she longed for she would have to do something about it herself. So, with the aid of a weekly gardening magazine, much practical hard work, and some gently persistent prodding of the males concerned, she achieved a lovely and original garden.

We children were rapturously delighted to stay on in the country. Besides all the fun of having a garden to play in and pets, I believe that young as we were, we had really missed, and almost craved for, the flowers, and colours and scents which we learnt at Groombridge to look on as a natural part of summer's happy constituents. I remember on hot summer days in London how I used to search anxiously in the dried-up grass in Kensington Gardens, always hoping I would find a daisy.

The mowing was done by donkey-power, Turner guiding the machine and the garden boy leading Jinny, the donkey, who wore little rubber overshoes for the job. Turner's wages were £1 a week.'

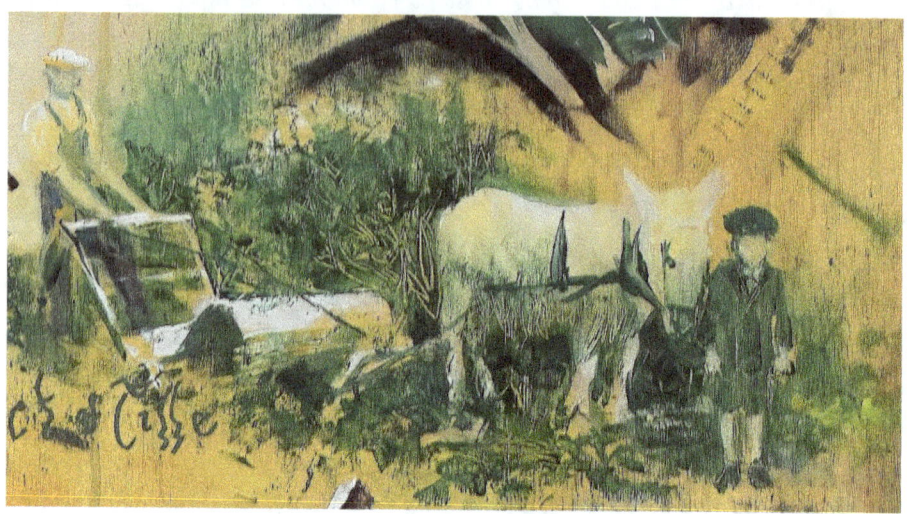

Which painting depicts Walter Turner the gardener, Jinny the donkey and the garden-boy? Can you discover what this painting is about? Do you think Walter Turner was paid a fair wage? Share your ideas about the differences in homes, lifestyles and gardens when Mary lived at Danecroft in 1918 and now. Can you find the painting which features Mary's father Brigadier General St. J. F. M. Fancourt C.B.? Why include his portrait on this painting?

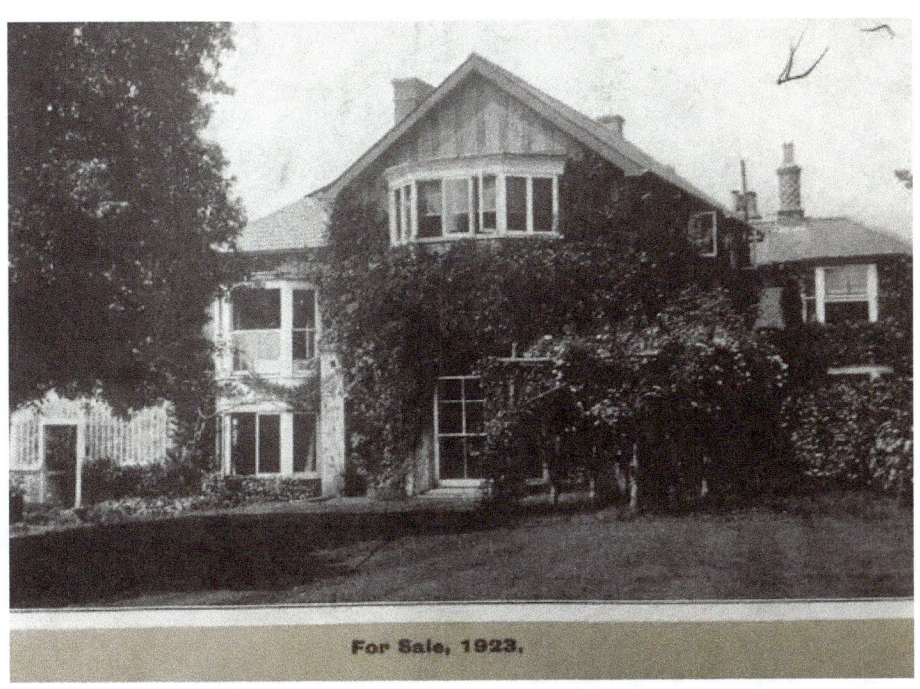

For Sale, 1923.

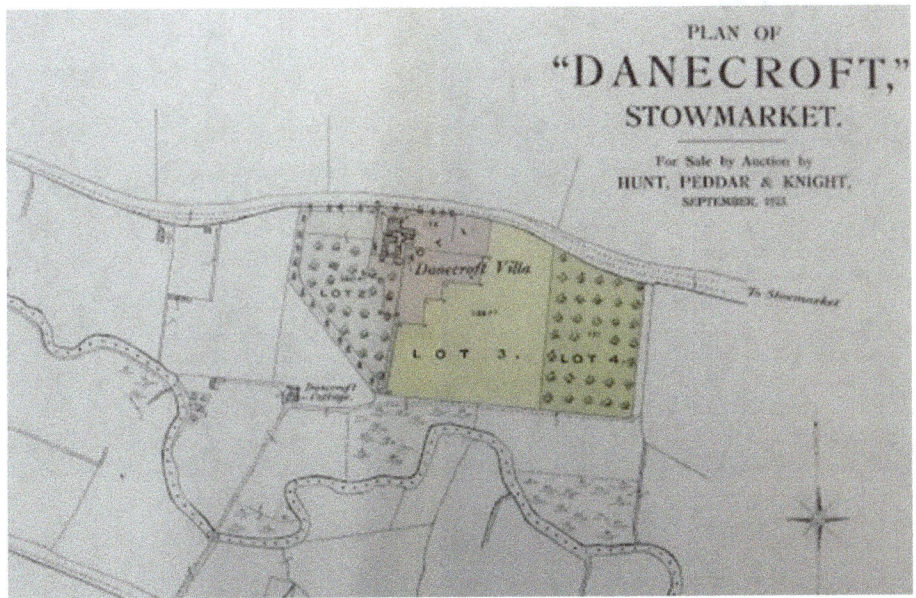

PLAN OF
"DANECROFT,"
STOWMARKET.

For Sale by Auction by
HUNT, PEDDAR & KNIGHT,
SEPTEMBER 1923

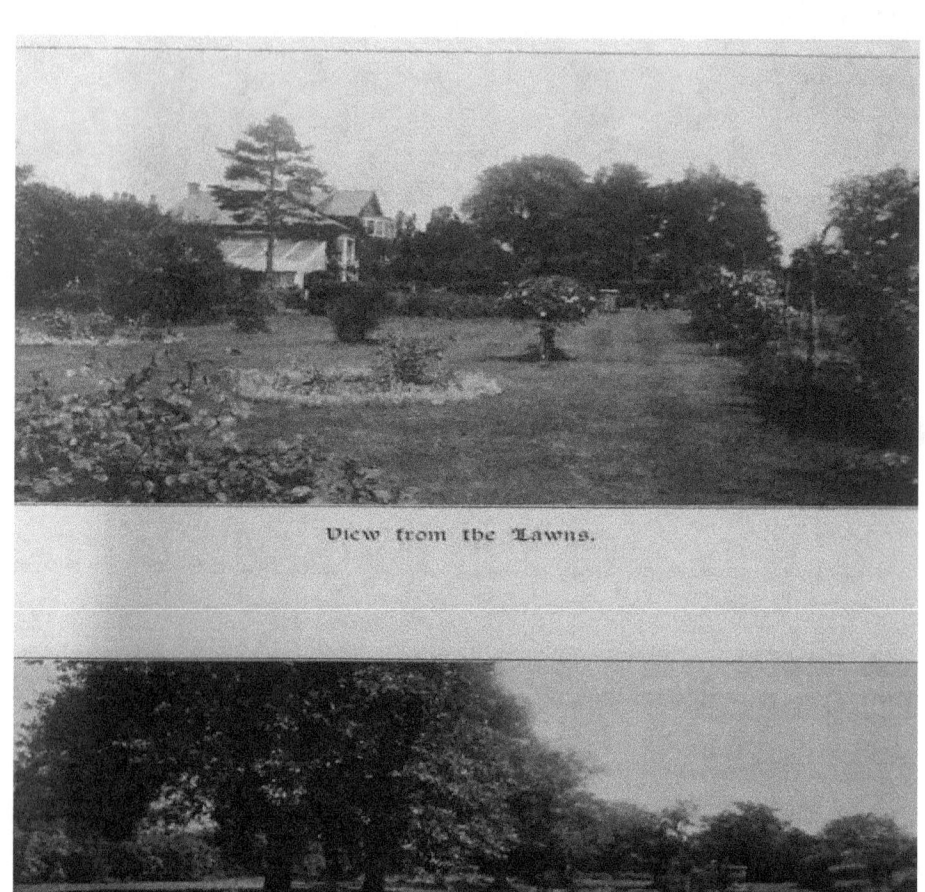

View from the Lawns.

17ft. 4in. x 11ft. 3in. fitted with open log grate and French casements to lean-to CONSERVATORY 16ft. 6in. x 13ft. 6in. with tiled floor, and heated by hot water pipes from boiler outside. MORNING ROOM having oak lined walls with shelving, 27ft. 6in. x 9ft. 9in. exclusive of 2 bay windows, fitted with modern grate, having tiled sides and hearth; lavatory basin, h. and c., door opening to lean-to Vinery and forcing house, 27ft. x 14ft., stocked with three prolific vines in full bearing. STUDY fitted with register grate. At the end of the hall is a Bathroom fitted h. and c., and W.C.

The Domestic Offices comprise :— Servants' Hall 12ft. 9in. x 8ft. 6in.; Kitchen 24ft. 6in. x 12ft. 9in. fitted with Eagle Range, dresser with cupboards, drawers with shelving, 3 cupboards, earthenware sink, h. and c. ; Pump and Well of excellent water; Scullery fitted with copper and shelving; Butler's Pantry fitted with 3 cupboards; Housemaid's Pantry with glazed sink, h. and c., and shelving.

On the First Floor approached by two staircases:—WORK ROOM 11ft. 6in. x 8ft. 4in. fitted with register grate, and 2 large store cupboards. EIGHT BEDROOMS measuring respectfully 25ft. 0in. x 10ft. 6in.; 17ft. 4in. x 10ft. 6in.; 15ft. 6in. x 12ft. 3in. ; 18ft. 9in. x 11ft.; 14ft. 9in. x 14ft. 3in. ; 13ft. 6in. x 8ft.; 12ft. x 10ft. 9in. and 10ft. 6in. x 10ft. 3in.; three are fitted with modern grates having tiled sides, and four with register grates. Bathroom h. and c., register grate and linen cupboard. Lavatory basin h. and c., and W.C.

At the Rear is :—A Range of Brick and Tiled buildings, comprising: Large Coal House, Potting House and Tool Shed, W.C.

The Stabling and Garage

include—Two Stall Stable, Harness Room and Two Coach Houses lined with match-boarding. Motor Garage, lined match-boarding with concrete floor, and paved washing yard, with pump and well of water. Timber and Corrugated Iron motor spirit store.

There is an excellent supply of good water from a well ; soft water well with pump, and the drainage is laid on modern principles.

The Grounds

are most tastefully laid out and comprise Gravel Paths, Rose Walks, Paved Garden, Flower Beds, Herbacious Borders, Full Sized Tennis Court and Grass Lawns studded with Rose Pergolas, well grown Shrubs, Ornamental Trees, Beech, Yew and Box Hedges, etc.

Kitchen Garden with Apple and Pear Trees.

Being Nos. 135 and parts of numbers 138 and 140 on the Ordnance Survey Map, and having an area of about

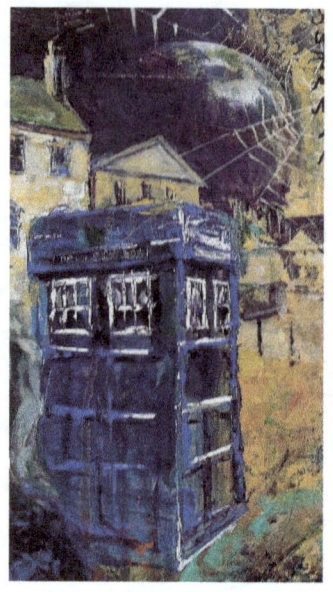
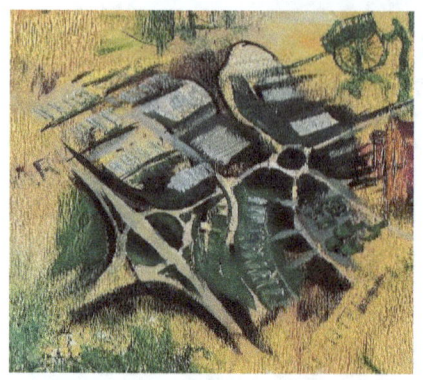
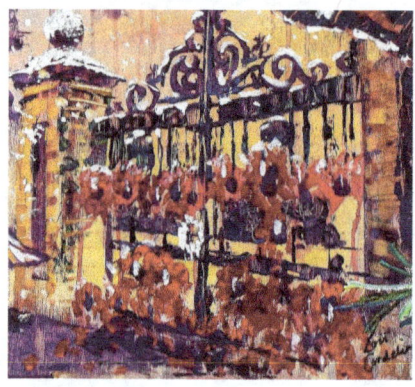

Do you recognise any of these places? Discover the painting they are on. If you were a time traveller where would you visit, who would you take with you and who would you meet?

People Links

Research led to discoveries of people from all walks of life as we glimpse through a window on the wider world through Danecroft Villa owners, their families and through other connections including • General John Scott KCB and C.B. • Alicia Scott • Adella Hutt • George Hutt • William Hutt • John Hutt • Charles Turner • Brigadier General St. J. F. M. Fancourt C.B. • Alfred E. Lewis • And more ………

Danecroft Villa owner (1852) Colonel John Scott KCB and C.B. was a British Army Officer in India. He served Queen Victoria as an Aide de Camp. Colonel John Scott died on 18 January 1873 while riding on Rotten

Row, Hyde Park, London. 'Fell of his horse going at walking pace and on rising was found to be dying.' The following promotion to take place consequent on death 'General John Scott. KCB, Colonel of the 7th Hussars'. Alicia Scott inherited Danecroft on the death of her husband. BRITISH ARMY OFFICER IN INDIA Brigadier General St. John F.M Fancourt C.B and J.P. and his family lived at Danecroft Villa between 1906 until his death in 1917 after his retirement from the Army. His distinguished career was in India primarily with the Bengal Lancers and in Intelligence. He was named in dispatches and thanked by the Government for his services on several occasions. He is buried in a prominent position at Harleston Church. His epitaph reads 'Let there be Light.' He has a brass plaque commemorating his life in Stowmarket Parish Church.

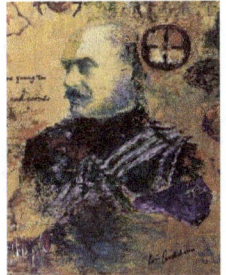

Brigadier General St. John F.M Fancourt C.B and J.P.

Search for the painting where he features and discover the painting title?

Where do you live? Find out about places, people and nature on your doorstep. Find out more about a subject that interests you.

A Sense of Place
Judith Thompson – Tinkler's Meadow

'I wanted to give voice to Tinkler's Meadow, a place that is a vital piece of the Stowmarket river-land tapestry which I love. It is my home, my settled and happy nature space. When I stand here I sense, feel and see people engaged in varying activities through time; different tribes travelling through this wildlife-rich river valley to hunt and to camp.

'Tinkler's meadow is a small field on the edge of town which welcomes people into Stowmarket where countryside meets the built environment. Tinkler's Meadow gently slopes towards the river at a precise location where river and land narrow, with a 1700's east-west turnpike road at its western boundary heading out of town towards Great Finborough and open countryside.

'The meadow was under attack by potential developers in 2017, and by giving it a voice I hoped to help to protect it. It seemed to me that the meadow was proud of its historical name and of being an important local green space for people, as well as a vital link through Rattlesden river valley, allowing wildlife and nature to thrive. Tinkler's Meadow asks to be a small field forever, and invites people to explore nature on their doorstep and discover more about Stowmarket's environment and heritage.'

Judith Thompson – Foreverland

Tinkler's Meadow
Is my name
Tithe Map number 255
Today, still the same

I am this field
I have a voice
No houses here
That's my choice

Come with me
Take my hand
To share and see
This Riverland

Judith Thompson – My Riverland

I am in the river valley, and upstream can see green riverbanks. I walk
here every day. Although vehicles rumble in the distance, my ear picks
out the early-morning bird song and the murmur of water sliding over
sand-covered shingle.

Footsteps follow a familiar time track. I love this early morning before
breakfast, when soft mist lifts and the meadow glistens in the rising sun,
and there's gentle colour all around.

Early autumn has a fresh, cool feel
with lingering light at the tail-end of day.

Soft earth beneath my feet,
faded summer grasses, bent to cast their seed,
traveller's joy and age-old hops combine.
Intertwined in new growth of elder and alder,
spiky blackberries catch lengthy, tangled shrubs.

At first familiar, the track is wide,
then grows mysterious as it narrows.
Arching tree-branch canopies protect me,
and the wild, indelible footprints,
hidden through layer upon layer
of endless time.

I love the calmness this wildness brings.
This place is a people's landscape.

A special place.

Mary Fancourt – Danecroft Days

This poem was written in 1970 for Mary's brother Henry St John Lockhart Fancourt on his 70th birthday. Mary writes, *'Those early years living in the country were full of delights to us children. Our greatest joy was provided by the little slow-flowing stream which meandered between water-meadows only just below our orchards. Perhaps a few verses I wrote last year for St, John on his seventieth birthday will give the best idea of our childhood's background in Suffolk.'*

When the century was young, and we were young too,
Memory brings back a store
Of gay, sunny pictures of meadows and woods
Just waiting for us to explore

In spring there were cowslips and buttercups gay,
And kingcups emblazoned the ditches,
While in Autumn the uplands were bright with ripe corn –
A landscape of warm golden riches

Beside our small river the dragonflies flew
Above banks where the water flowers bloomed
The proud mother moorhen led out her chicks,
And the snipe up above dived and boomed

Dappled shadows disclosed the swarms of small fish-
Or sometimes a sleek water rat
At the meadow's far fringe saucy rabbits popped out
To spruce up their whiskers and chat

In hedgerows and tree trunks the birds built their nests
A goal for sharp eyes to espy,
Violets and five-fingers smothered the woods
With a magic that made time fly

Then as dinner-time neared, a quick scurry home
Brought explorers on time to their places,
The sirloin was carved, and starched, kindly maids
Handed plates round with smiling faces

With winter, the garden in Christmas-white guise
Presented a sparkling call
Then back to the fireside to make buttered toast
And with evergreens deck out the hall

Of course there were dull days, rebellions and tears,
But how faded they've grown with time!
It's the happy bright days which reach over the years,
They're the ones on which memories shine

Steve Williams (1950 to 2020) – Oi Wuz Bawn An Bred In Sarfulk

Stowmarket local archivist, Steve Williams, was a splendid creative spirit. Judith and Stephen became friends during the 2020 lockdown when Steve joined the Stow Stories research team. Steve wrote songs and was a keen artist, poet and cartoonist (he loved everything about the Giles family created by cartoonist Carl Giles at the end of World War II). During the worst times of Covid in 2020 Steve re-wrote the lyrics to many classic songs and Judith complied a songbook for him entitled 'Covid 2019 Songbook and More'. This is lodged in The Hold (Suffolk Archives). Steve's love of Stowmarket and Suffolk are reflected in his changed words of the Bee Gee song Ellan Vannin.

Oi wuz bawn an bred in Sarfulk
An it's shaped we as oi've growen.
An we're blessed with much more sunloight
Than the rest the country's known.

Chorus –
Ower accent gets much derision!
Still oi'm proud as proud can be.
To be part uv dear ol' Sarfulk
From Heathland to ol' Norf sea!

Haps we ain't got no tall mountains
But we've got ower Sarfulk skies!
An the locals are all friendly.
The may talk slow but they're wise.

Chorus-
Ower accent gets much derision!
Still oi'm proud as proud can be.

To be part uv dear ol' Sarfulk
From Heathland to ol' Norf sea!
If moi loife should end tomorrow
No more to walk ower pebbled shore.
Some will look on me with envy
Cuz oi was Sarfulk to the core!

July 28th, 2020
Steve Williams – The Bored Bard

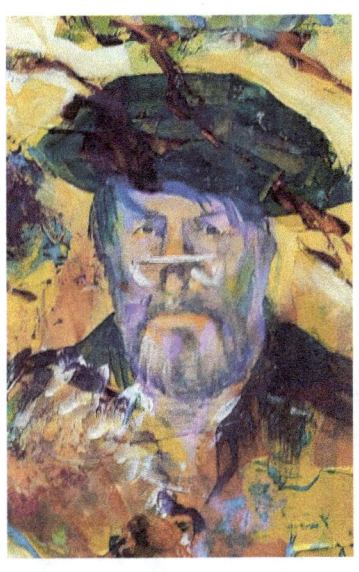

Would you like to be a creative spirit like Steve? Try writing, drawing or painting a subject you care about. Share what you have achieved with friends.

Henry David Thoreau – 'Time is but a stream.'

Judith writes, 'For me this writing captures the beauty and uniqueness of planet earth within the vast universe. Our time here matters.'

Time is but a stream

Time is but the stream I go a-fishing in. I drink at it; but, while I drink I see a sandy bottom and detect how shallow it is. Its thin current slides away, but eternity remains. I would drink deeper; fish in the sky, whose bottom is pebbly with stars. I cannot count one. I know not the first letter of the alphabet. I have always been regretting that I was not as wise as the day I was born.

On the Bicentennial of Thoreau's birth (July 12, 2017) Tom Montgomery Fate shared his thoughts on Henry David Thoreau – 'Time is but a stream'. (Tom is an author and professor of creative writing and literature courses).

'Because the heart of fishing is not catching. The heart of fishing is waiting and watching—for a bite or nibble from whatever comes along—be it a pickerel or a pout, or, perhaps, an act of love, or forgiveness. Thoreau waits and watches amid the quiet stream of time—of consciousness, of patience, of attentiveness. Perhaps one clear night Thoreau saw the stars reflected on the surface of the Concord River or against the pebbly bottom of Walden Pond— the convergence of sky and earth in the water. Maybe he was trying to dream of the world beyond the moving water, to drink deeper, to believe in the unseen, and the kind of time that cannot be measured. Not numeric time— what the Greeks call chronos—not those four 60-second increments between 9:11 and 9:15 a.m. But kairos time, an immeasurable unending moment, like the moment where that same river enters the ocean, and suddenly, yet completely, becomes a part of the whole. Thoreau's river of time is defined not by numbers but by relationships, by belonging to the river, to the stars, the sand and fish. It connects the human animal to the whole of Creation. I call this natural time.'

Judith Thompson - Web of my Life

'I was inspired to distil my awe, wonder and experience of nature into Web of My Life, where I do feel 'at home'.'

Single feather
A wing
Insect sting
All manner of unusual things

Otter's tail
Snail's trail
Fox paw-print
Clue or hint

Water vole whisker
Buzzard beak
Barn owl eyes
Many a surprise

Kingfisher flash
Spiderlings dash
River and land
Like sea and sand

Shy Moorhen
Badgers' den
Ant, grub, worm, beetle, fly
Live, then die

Rivers flow
Root, shoot, leaf, flower
Care, protect
Interconnect

Sunlight, rain
Seed and grain
Soil, plant
Emerge again

Planet earth
Stardust
Water, fire, air
Ether

Moon, sun
Milky Way
My web
My Home

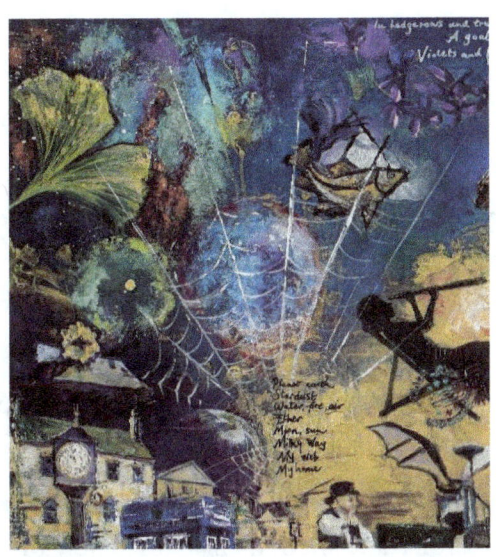

An image from the painting Home In The Universe

Note: 'Web of my Life' has also been published in the book *Wild Seas, Wilder Cities* and online at pensoftheearth.co.uk. 'Danecroft Otter,' Judith's account of rescuing an otter kit, is also published in *Wild Seas, Wilder Cities*. Details on how to purchase *Wild Seas, Wilder Cities* are available at: pensoftheearth.co.uk/the-book

People Links:

Mary St. John Fancourt (1898 to 2002) lived with her family at Danecroft Villa. She was a Stowmarket Land Girl, author, poet, and became a creative reference for the storytelling paintings. Her father, Brigadier-General St. John Michell Fancourt (1847 - 1917) is commemorated by a brass plaque in St Peter's and St Mary's Church in the centre of Stowmarket He was appointed Companion, Order of the Bath (C.B.) and held the office of Justice of the Peace (J.P.). He gained the rank of Brigadier-General in the Bengal Lancers. Mary's brother, Captain Henry St. John Lockhart Fancourt (1990 - 2003) fought in the Battle of Jutland on 31 May 1916. He was awarded the Distinguished Service Order (D.S.O.) He gained the rank of Captain in the Royal Navy. The whole family had incredible life stories.

Henry Fancourt – Imperial War Museum, London

In 1960 to celebrate her brother's 70th birthday, Mary wrote a poem about her childhood memories of her life at Danecroft Villa. Verses of her poem relate to each of the eight large paintings and resonate with Judith's 27 years' of living near to Danecroft Villa, Mary's home in Stowmarket.

'Those early years living in the country were full of delights to us children. Our greatest joy was provided by the little slow-flowing stream which meandered between water-meadows only just below our orchards.'

The researchers discovered that Danecroft Villa, cottage and land connected some extraordinary extremes of wealth, occupation, and social class over a period of 378 years between 1618 and 1996.

This included: royalty, high society; landed gentry; honoured renowned servicemen; successful tradesmen such as maltster, brewer, farmer, hop grower, osier farmer, tomato nursery foreman, florist, and a mechanical engineer. We found a teacher, dressmaker, cook, parlour maid, auctioneer, bank manager, mathematician, Charles Turner, a grocer and draper; country folk and a labourer; John Finter, a market gardener and his family. Brigadier General St. John Michell Fancourt, Captain Henry St. John Lockhart Fancourt, and Mary St. John Fancourt were discovered along with Samuel Girling, Thomas Barnes and Major Lewis.

Then even more people were uncovered: solicitors, lawyers, including William Strickland Cookson who represented William Wordsworth; a liberal politician of a high order, William Hutt, who was Vice-President of the Board of Trade, and Paymaster-General, 1860-5. P.C., 1860. K.C.B., 1865. He negotiated a treaty of commerce between Great Britain and Austria, 1863 and was a member of the Commission at Vienna to examine the Austrian tariff. We found a Commissioner for the foundation of South Australia and a member of the New Zealand Company, who was instrumental in annexing those islands to Great Britain.

This list could go on and on as there were many more individuals and families of interest and intrigue..

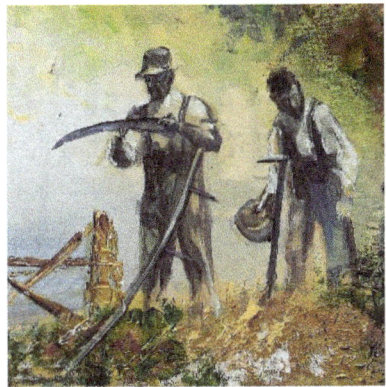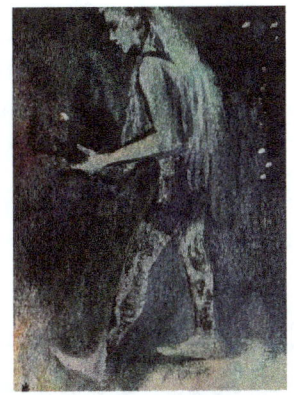

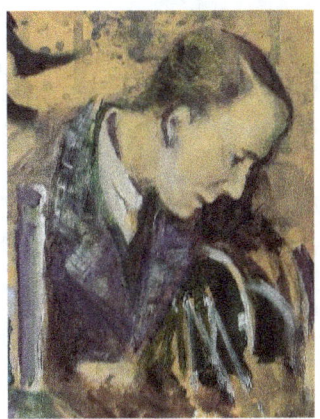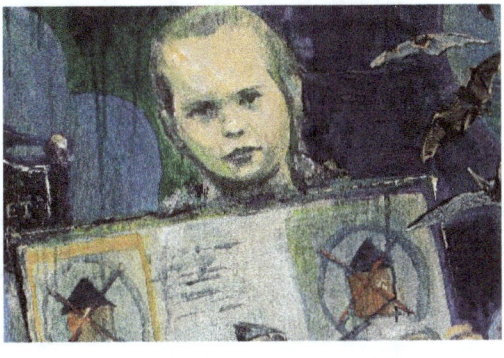

Which paintings feature the people above? What you think they are doing and why?

Nature Links:

Stowmarket sits at the junction of two rivers, the Rattlesden and the Gipping. Both have influenced the growth of this historic market town by nurturing the raw materials for the industries that developed here. There is evidence of extraordinary biodiversity in Stowmarket river valleys, but nowadays nature needs our help.

Foreverland Mural

A collaboration between artist Loïs Cordelia and local resident Judith Thompson. Loïs created the mural largely inspired by Judith's poem

Foreverland which is woven into the riverland map in the centre, managing to squeeze in fifty-one species of animals, trees, plants and fungi, sculpting each one using modelling paste and palette knives, and then bringing it to life with iridescent acrylic paint colours. This mural design celebrates the extraordinary biodiversity of the Rivers Rattlesden in 2021 and the Gipping before canalisation as the Ipswich and Stowmarket Navigation in 1793.

In the Reverend A G H Hollingsworth's book The History of Stowmarket (1844) he states:

"... down to the year 1790 the Gipping presented a scene of quiet beauty, peculiarly English, undisturbed, and partaking of the gentle features of the richly wooded park, or verdant farm. .... as if the river loved to dream ..."

Stowmarket's two rivers led to the town's growth and prosperity through the ages and this mural especially reflects the rich biodiversity currently evident along the River Rattlesden valley. This valuable wildlife corridor which provides a mosaic of habitats is worth protecting and especially now when we are coming to realise that so much wildlife is under mortal threat.

Fifty-one species are listed in the key below.

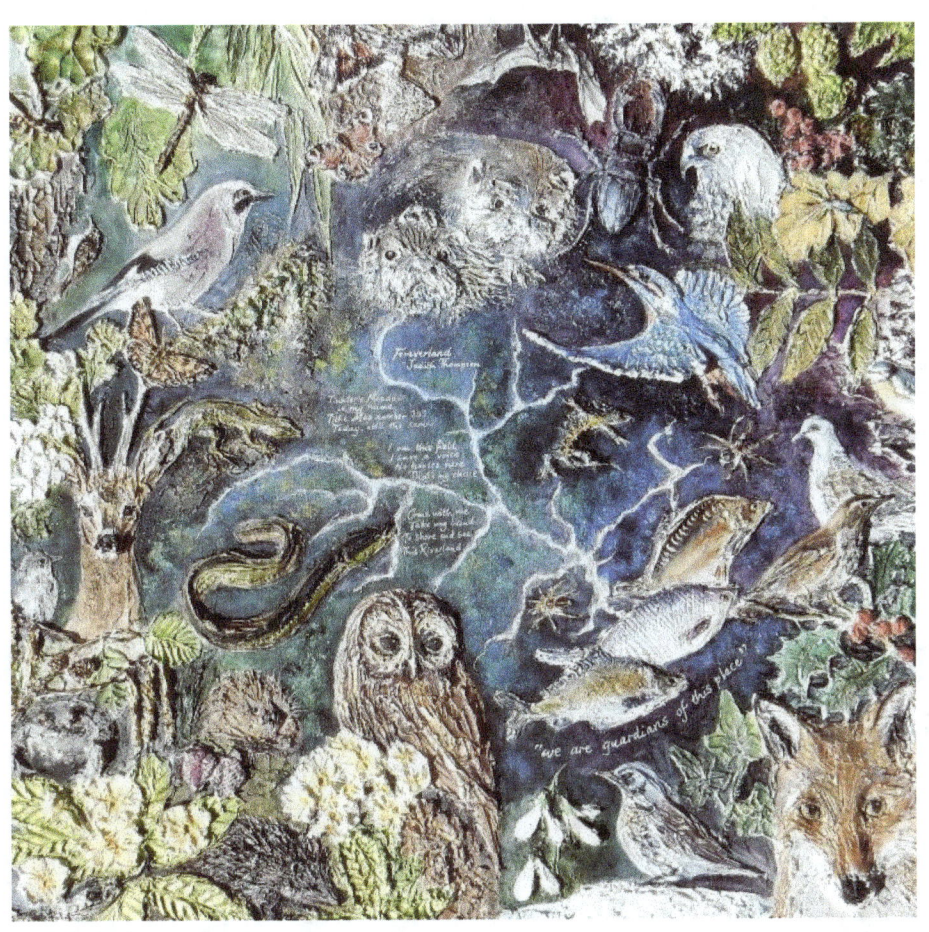

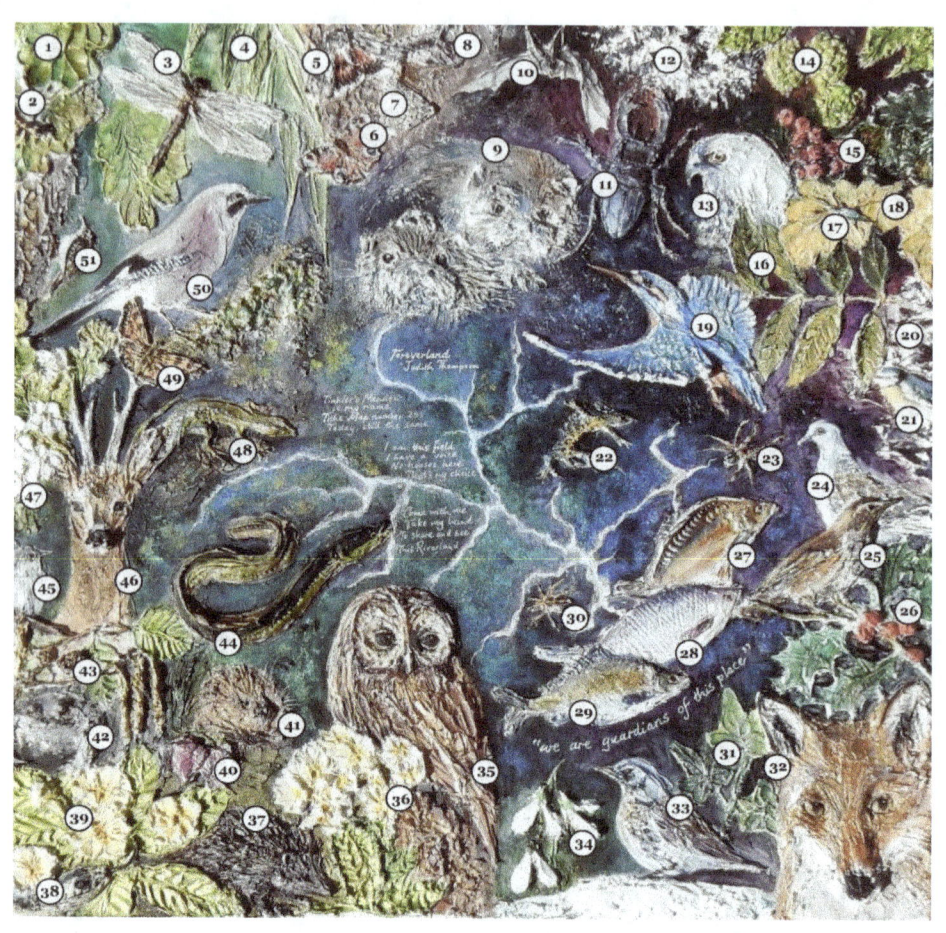

1) Oak Quercus robur

2) Weevil Hunting Wasp Cerceris arenaria

3) Brown Hawker Dragonfly - Aeshena grandis

4) Osier Willow Salix viminalis

5) Red Underwing moth Catocala nupta

6) Peacock Butterfly Aglais io

7) Clifden Nonpareil moth Catocala fraxini

8) Oak Beauty moth Biston strataria

9) Pair of Otters (including one that was rescued by Judith Thompson) Lutra lutra

10) Brown Long-eared Bat Plecotus auritus

11) Stag Beetle Lucanus cervus

12) Coral Tooth Fungus Hericium coralloides

13) Sparrowhawk Accipiter nisus

14) Common Hop Humulus lupulus

15) Hawthorn Crataegus monogyna

16) Ash Fraxinus excelsior

17) Musk Beetle Lampyris noctiluca

18) Oak Quercus robur

19) Kingfisher Alcedo atthis

20) Turkeytail Fungus Trametes versicolor

21) Blue Tit Cyanistes caeruleus

22) Great Crested Newt Triturus cristatus

23) Silky Gallows Spider Phycosoma inornatum

24) Turtle Dove Streptopelia turtur

25) Redwing Turdus iliacus

26) Holly Ilex aquifolium

27) Mirror Carp Cyprinus carpio carpio

28) Common Bream Abramis brama

29) Common Carp Cyprinus carpio

30) Yellow Striped Bear Spider Arctosa fulvolineata

31) Ivy Hedera helix

32) Red Fox Vulpes vulpes

33) Fieldfare Turdus pilaris

34) Snowdrop Galanthus nivalis

35) Tawny Owl Strix aluco

36) Oxlip Primula elatior

37) Hedgehog Erinaceus europaeus

38) Barred Grass Snake Natrix helvetica

39) Primrose Primula vulgaris

40) Snake's Head Fritillary Fritillaria meleagris

41) Water Vole Arvicola amphibius

42) Common Toad Bufo bufo

43) Alder Alnus glutinosa

44) Eel Anguilla anguilla

45) Spotted Flycatcher Muscicapa striata

46) Roe Deer Capreolus capreolus

47) Hawthorn Crataegus monogyna

48) Common Lizard Zootoca vivipara

49) Comma Butterfly Polygonia c-album

50) Jay Garrulus glandarius

51) Tree Creeper Certhia familiaris

www.youtube.com/@Walksandwanders

www.youtube.com/@LoisCordelia

www.loiscordelia.com

Danecroft Otter

In 'The Danecroft Otter,' written by Judith Thompson and published by Pens of the Earth, Judith reflects on Danecroft and its rich diversity: "Our life here is like living at a film location. This is a magical 9.5-acre place; a rare mosaic of forgotten abandoned habitat of both dry and wet woodland: part remains untouched since the second world war. Diverse tall plants – sedge, butterbur and purple-headed reed co-exist without dominance, each suited to different areas and conditions. Two thousand years ago, this was swamp land; two hundred years ago, it was farmed for hop, then for willow osiers. 80 years ago, it became war-time derelict land. Rattlesden river is ever the constant, meandering through."

'The Danecroft Otter' is Judith's true story of an otter kit rescue on Danecroft land.

Video: You can see one of the otters being released here: https://youtu.be/aET1_9KoWZc

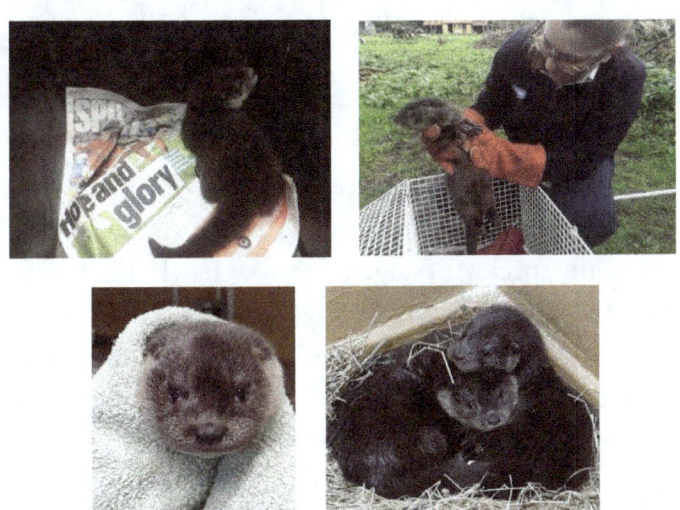

Inspiration: I wrote this following the magical encounter my husband and I had with an abandoned otter. We are fortunate to own 9.5 acres of land. We knew otters visited the river and pond from time to time by the evidence of fish scales, tracks, and spraint. Having this close encounter with such a small, isolated, frightened, wide-eyed, wild animal was a heart-stopping experience which led me to record the otter events as they unfolded during the day.

'The Danecroft Otter' is available to read in the Kindle e-book of *Wild Seas, Wilder Cities* now available from Amazon.co.uk.

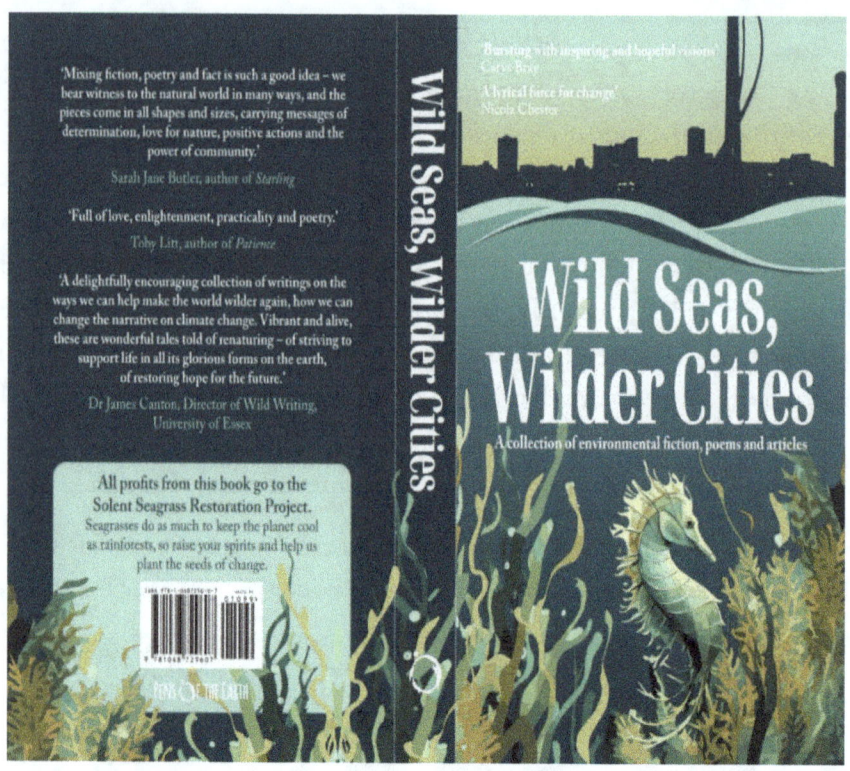

The cover of the book shows text including:

'Mixing fiction, poetry and fact is such a good idea – we bear witness to the natural world in many ways, and the pieces come in all shapes and sizes, carrying messages of determination, love for nature, positive actions and the power of community.'

Sarah Jane Butler, author of *Starling*

'Full of love, enlightenment, practicality and poetry.'

Toby Litt, author of *Patience*

'A delightfully encouraging collection of writings on the ways we can help make the world wilder again, how we can change the narrative on climate change. Vibrant and alive, these are wonderful tales told of renaturing – of striving to support life in all its glorious forms on the earth, of restoring hope for the future.'

Dr James Canton, Director of Wild Writing, University of Essex

All profits from this book go to the Solent Seagrass Restoration Project. Seagrasses do as much to keep the planet cool as rainforests, so raise your spirits and help us plant the seeds of change.

'Bursting with inspiring and hopeful visions' Carys Bray

'A lyrical force for change.' Nicola Chester

Wild Seas, Wilder Cities

A collection of environmental fiction, poems and articles

A significant number of protected species live in or depend on habitats in the Rattlesden river valley including Otter, Water vole, Great Crested Newts, Bats (eight species), Badger, Sparrow hawk, Kestrel, Tawny owl, Song thrush, Mistle thrush, Grey Wagtail, and several species of moth. Many are a priority species and are fully protected under schedule 5 of the Wildlife and Countryside Act 1981. Many are named Priority Species under the UK Post-2010 Biodiversity Framework.

A number of videos are part of a special Walks and Wanders series, filmed in collaboration with Steve and Judith Thompson, the owners of Danecroft, who manage their land in a way that provides diverse habitat for wildlife to thrive. The links are also in the Appendix.

'Food Web' sculpture, Spring 2022 - Artist Loïs Cordelia

Stowmarket's Food Museum looks after a 1.8km stretch of the river Rattlesden from its source near Felsham to where it joins the river Gipping in Stowmarket. In spring 2022 a series of sculptures was unveiled inspired by the natural world along a 1km pathway which meanders along the river. Loïs Cordelia's 'Web of Life' was one of these.

Loïs Cordelia's spectacular and intricate three-dimensional spider's web spans several metres and rewards exploration. The impressive wire sculpture design symbolises the interconnectedness of living things through a food web, with a specific emphasis on the rich biodiversity of the Rattlesden river valley.

Loïs explained: 'It's made of wire and food-related items. Wire represents the interconnectedness of all things. Metal cutlery and kitchen utensils emphasise the theme of food in reference both to the food web and the Food Museum.'

Loïs Cordelia has sculpted using wire for nearly 30 years. You can discover more about the artist and about this sculpture via these links:

www.youtube.com/@LoisCordelia

www.loiscordelia.com

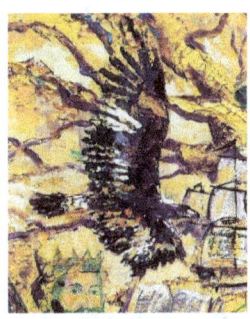 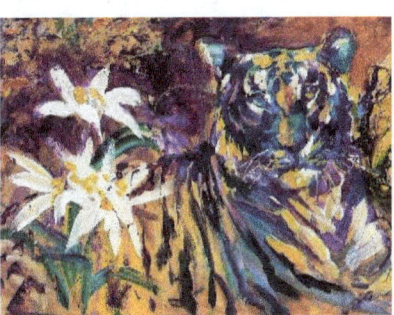 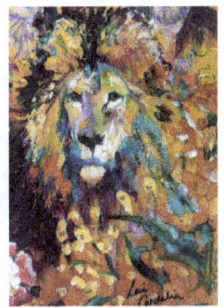

Discover which painting includes these three wild animals. Share your thoughts about why they are included? Have a go to identify more nature images on this painting?

Reflections

Judith as Researcher:

"I am proud of the Tinkler's Quest legacy. Our research and Loïs Cordelia's superb storytelling paintings promote a collective responsibility to protect and cherish the place where we live, the communities around us and the nature on our doorstep. Loïs's unique painting style perfectly interprets the research content and invites people to discover and explore Stowmarket in a new way.

"For me as a story researcher the journey from a campaign to save Tinkler's Meadow, through the Stow Stories research, to arrival at the launch of Tinkler's Quest art trail, video and book has been testing, rewarding and heart-warming. In sharing my ambition, I connect with other individuals and organisations to advocate for a kinder society, and to encourage community action for a more sustainable, greener future."

Loïs as Artist:

"Creating the Tinkler's Quest series of paintings has been an extraordinary challenge, a journey through time and space, and one of the biggest projects I've ever attempted.

"Collaborating closely with researcher Judith Thompson throughout, I sought to condense a wealth of Stowmarket related references, imagery and anecdotes into a series of artworks that were meaningful, layered and full of intrigue.

"I hope that my paintings will inspire conversations, more research, and discoveries – as you join us on Tinkler's Quest, we walk in the footsteps of time as guardians of this place."

Author - Judith Thompson
Creative Campaigner for nature

Throughout her professional life Judith has been involved in education in many different guises, with a love of supporting others – young and older, of all abilities – to believe in themselves and to discover their strengths and talents. For the last 28 years she has lived in a quiet nature place that is full of wonder. She is a creative campaigner, eco activist, project volunteer and – her favourite job of all – a land girl working alongside her husband to protect, preserve and enhance their patch of land that nestles within the Rattlesden river valley for the short time they act as its guardians.

PART 4

What you can do

Stow Stories and Tinkler's Quest promote an ethos of caring about our environment. Together we can combat climate change through words, creativity and local action wherever we live.

Tinkler's Quest painting content has wide appeal for individuals, community groups and organisations to use to link their activities to the paintings. Inspire research, join a group, become a volunteer or plan a creative personal or community project and have fun. Video and e-book content can be tailored to specific interests, ages and abilities. They are designed to make the Tinkler's Quest art trail accessible and to be used in a supportive environment such as a care home, a community well-being group or with those affected by loneliness, depression, isolation or loss.

Explore outdoors on foot, online or in your mind.

Be inspired to connect to your environment and heritage in a new and different way.

What gives you a sense of place? Give yourself an unhurried time in a place which you already know, slowing down to notice sensations: what can you hear, feel, touch, smell, taste? walking slowly, hands free, as you allow yourself to be drawn by intrigue, noticing tiny details you have previously missed, allowing your feet and not your mind to lead the way.

– Where do you go to be quiet?
– Where do you go to lift your spirit?
– What does home mean to you?
– Have you ever taken your shoes off and walked on the earth, or paddled in the river or sea? What sensations come to mind?
– Do you have a favourite tree, or rock, or bend in the river, or patch of sky?
– When you sit here, in this place, what speaks to you without words?
– Where are your roots?

Have a go at free writing

Put down anything which comes to you without alteration or criticism, then turn the page and leave what you have written to lie fallow for a few days before reading it and selecting the words and phrases which sing to you of your place upon the earth.

Have a good read

Ranger Hamza, from CBeebies' Let's Go For a Walk gave us all sorts of ideas for walking adventures www.bbc.co.uk/tiny-happy-people/articles/zt3rg7h

Top tips for being more outdoorsy.

Person by person, street by street, we need to repair our connection to nature. Search for 'Encounter Nature' in the App Store in the UK, Ireland or Google Play Store. Encounter is a free, guided nature journal from nature writer Melissa Harrison that will open your eyes to your nearby wild, whether you live in the heart of a city or the deepest countryside. Find out more at www.encounter-nature.com

Follow the Stowmarket Sprites.

Stow Stories partnered with the Literacy Trust to create an interactive Tinkler's Quest Trail based on the Storytelling paintings. www.literacytrust. org.uk/communities/suffolk/summer-story-trails-in-suffolk

Create - What you can do

Loïs thinks a map is a magic carpet for the mind. Create your own map. Have fun on your own or with friends when you create a map, include aspects from history, landscape and the environment. Where are you? Add buildings, wildlife, people, transport, add a line or two of writing, add a bit of magic and perhaps a Sprite. (look at the painting Settlement or Round and About for inspiration)

Judith thinks nature spaces like the Rattlesden river valley and Tinkler's Meadow are so special information about them should be shared and protected.

– Gather information about place, people and nature in your favourite nature space. Create a picture or collage by using paint, photos or fabrics. Look closely at the paintings Reflect and Hope, River and Land, A Greener Future for inspiration.

– Take a look at 'Home in the Universe' or 'Round and About,' choose a title - what would you include to create your own picture inspired by the title.

– On your Tree of Life – who or what would you choose to be on your tree and what images of place, people and nature would you include? Look at the painting 'Pushing Boundaries - Earth Champions,' research any of the names to find out what they have done. A super group activity.

– What would you include a world wide web of information and imagery? Look at the painting 'Web of Lifelines' for inspiration. Get creative, perhaps have a go with textiles to create a response.

– Reflect on your memories and record in some way emotions and experiences you have had or know about, or look to the future and what would you like to see or do in or beyond planet earth. The painting 'Life Goes On' celebrates sad and happy events through time.

– Interpret aspects of any painting or their titles through dance, drama, music or song. www.nature.org/en-us/what-we-do/our-priorities/tackle-climate-change/climate-change-stories/climate-change-songs

Create in Loïs Cordelia style?
Search for:
DIY Palette Knife Tutorial
Creative Coffee Painting
Fun with Freestyle Papercutting
Foliate faces
On www.youtube.com/@LoisCordelia

Loïs says ' I seize every opportunity to reference environmental themes in my artwork and spread awareness. The Green Man or foliate face is a recurring symbol, as is the spider's web

Stowmarket Garden Project – Stitching Stow
www.youtube.com/@SuffolkLibraries
Weaving a giant food web for the Food Museum in Stowmarket
www.loiscordelia.com/blog

Other ideas
A number of people from different occupations pre-viewed the video and shared ideas of how they would use the content.

Which part/s of the video would you use as a creative learning resource?
'Leader or teacher watch the video, then choose an aspect relevant to their group. Coming at this from the perspective of sharing it with those who would not be familiar with Stowmarket I would focus on the geography aspects of the film, particularly in regard to the fact that Stowmarket has such wonderful greenspace in such a condensed area, especially comparatively to North America. I also would focus on the section where Judith speaks about how home is where you are at the time. This is especially relevant for international viewers.'

How might you use the questions about each painting in the film and within concept texts below? Please suggest appropriate questions for your group.
'I can see that a set of cards, (or pausing video or book) with one painting on each, that children could discuss and explore first in a small group or pair would be very interesting. The image would generate much speculation and language (what's this picture about .... who is in it .... what story could it be telling ...). Then linking the painting to the idea or facts behind each one, perhaps visiting any linked Stowmarket Place (on foot or online). Thinking and talking about conservation, protecting the environment, then discussing

the concept of a campaign – why would someone do that? So many inspiring images to find the best way into personal / group research and action. What can we do to nurture a place we care about? Could all of the paintings as a collection be lent to local schools or groups?

'I would suggest asking international viewers to reflect on what do they know about the local area they themselves live on. How much history do they know regarding where their home was built or significant landmarks in town? Do they know any interesting stories about where they live? What does their town mean to them? Or does it at all? If not, how come?'

'In regard to the specific paintings, I would be interested to know by viewers which was their favourite and why. I think this would be especially interesting from the perspective of those who have not visited before. Perhaps they can then see their own surroundings reflected in the art that was made to represent a town on the other side of the earth.'

Explore and discover joy in nature - take a look and try something new

Loïs Cordelia - Community artist, speed-painter, illustrator, demonstrator and tutor, based in Sanquhar, UK.
www.loiscordelia.com

Saving the small things that run the planet
www.buglife.org.uk

Earth Education - We believe earth education is a serious task but getting to know the natural world is a lifelong adventure full of wonderful experiences and joy.
www.eartheducation.org.uk

Gordon MacLellan – Creeping Toad – is one of Britain's leading environmental art and education workers. Take a look at the Toadblog:
www.creepingtoad.blogspot.com
www.findschoolworkshops.co.uk/Primary/Author-illustrator-Visits

The National Education Nature Park is a UK programme which empowers children and young people to make a positive difference to both their own and nature's future. www.educationnaturepark.org.uk www.educationnaturepark.org.uk/resources www.educationnaturepark.org.uk/resource/hidden-nature-challenge

Kids for Saving Earth - Help Kids Help our Earth - Education into Action Curriculum. Clint was different. He didn't just wonder. He acted. He started a club for kids, dedicated to peaceful Earth-saving actions. The first club was in his school, Sunny Hollow Elementary in New Hope, Minnesota.
www.kidsforsavingearth.org

Greenpeace UK - Free educational resources for schools, youth groups, parents, carers and young people. Explore environmental challenges and be inspired to act!
www.greenpeace.org.uk/resource-hub/education-resources

Our mission is to encourage stewardship of rivers and watersheds and to nurture the next generation of civic and conservation leaders by engaging the creative ...
www.clearingmagazine.org/anthology

PART 5

The Journey to the Paintings

Stow Stories to Tinkler's Quest

The journey to discover and share the history of Stowmarket and the Rattlesden river valley, to celebrate its present and protect its future, was first inspired by a campaign to prevent two speculative building proposals.

2017 – Destruction of natural wildlife habitat (Ecocide) led to a campaign to stop housing development

A small field, historically named Tinkler's Meadow, forms a vital part of the designated river Rattlesden Special Landscape Area. Tinkler's Meadow abuts Danecroft land to the west. Sitting at a vital landscape pinch point between the river Rattlesden and Finborough Road, close to the town's boundary, Tinkler's Meadow provides a vital link through Rattlesden river valley, allowing wildlife and nature to thrive. It is hugely significant to biodiversity, to local people and to the wider community.

Despite this land being outside Stow's settlement boundary, in 2018, two speculative building proposals were made by developers who wanted to build houses on this land. Local campaigners collaborated with Councillors and other professionals to resist the development. As part of this ongoing resistance, the idea of Stow Stories was born.

To date the development of Tinkler's Meadow has not taken place.

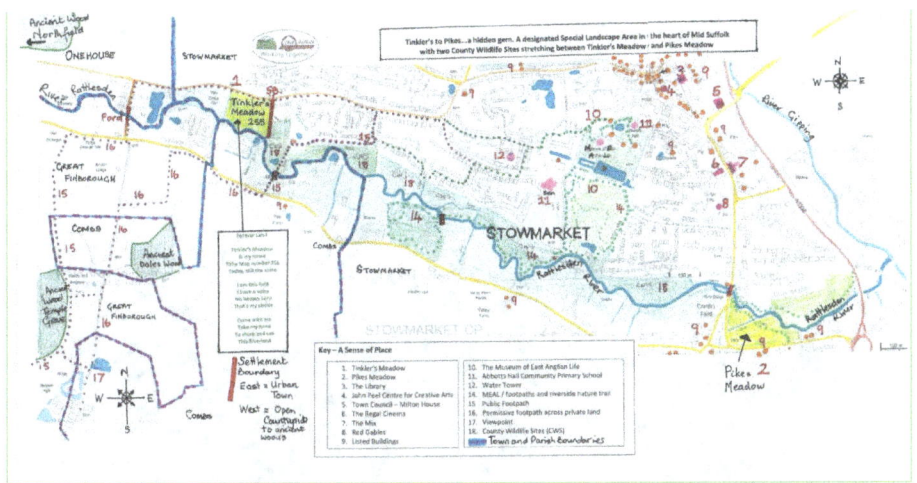

Danecroft – an historical note

Until 1960, a splendid residence, Danecroft Villa, with renowned nursery gardens was a popular place to buy tomatoes, play tennis or promenade among the flowers and trees when the garden was open to the public.

Fact or flight of fancy? Archaeological excavations unearthed pre-historic evidence at Danecroft Villa. Danes were believed to have an encampment in Stowmarket on the road leading to Finborough, '*where the meadows slope down to the rivulet, near to the hop grounds and nursery garden at Danecroft.*' Quote by Rev A. G. H. Hollingsworth M.A. 1844 in his book 'The History of Stowmarket'

It seems possible that Tinkler's Meadow might well have been home to such an encampment.

Danecroft Villa no longer stands.

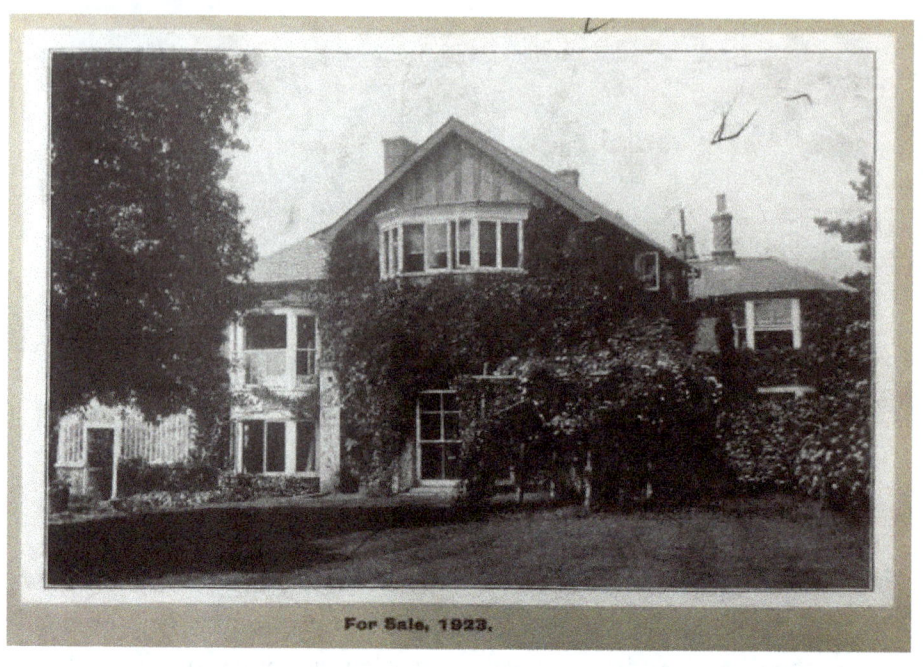

For Sale, 1923.

Historic Danecroft land remains a significant part of the rich mosaic of habitats which make the river Rattlesden valley vitally important when it comes to protecting the UK's endangered wildlife, such as otters, water voles and great crested newts.

Such is the rarity of otters they are a priority species in the UK Biodiversity Action Plan and are classified as Near Threatened on the IUCN Red List (2004). They are fully protected in the UK under schedule 5 of the Wildlife and Countryside Act 1981. Read more about the presence of otters in the Rattlesdon River valley in 'Danecroft Otter', by Judith Thomspon, published by Pens of the Earth. www.pensoftheearth.co.uk/danecroft-otter

2018 Stow Stories and the Rattlesden River Valley Network

Saving Tinkler's Meadow was the start and remains and the heart of Stow Stories. The community objection campaign gradually transformed into two new projects to strengthen objections to future speculative proposals. Stow Stories environment and heritage project and the Rattlesden River Valley Network. Both campaigns seek to raise awareness and act to promote a greener future.

Stow Stories:

Stow stories sought to enable people to learn more about where they lived, create their own responses to that place, and share their work as widely as possible. In 2018, Suffolk Archives ran a countywide programme of activities to complement the development of The Hold. One of the largest parts of this programme was Sharing Suffolk Stories. Judith Thompson successfully applied for Stow Stories to be included in this project which ran until 2022. Participants were supported to delve into archive collections to uncover unique stories about the people, places and events of their county. The Hold is now a thriving archive venue on the Ipswich waterfront.
www.suffolkarchives.co.uk/about-suffolk-archives/the-hold

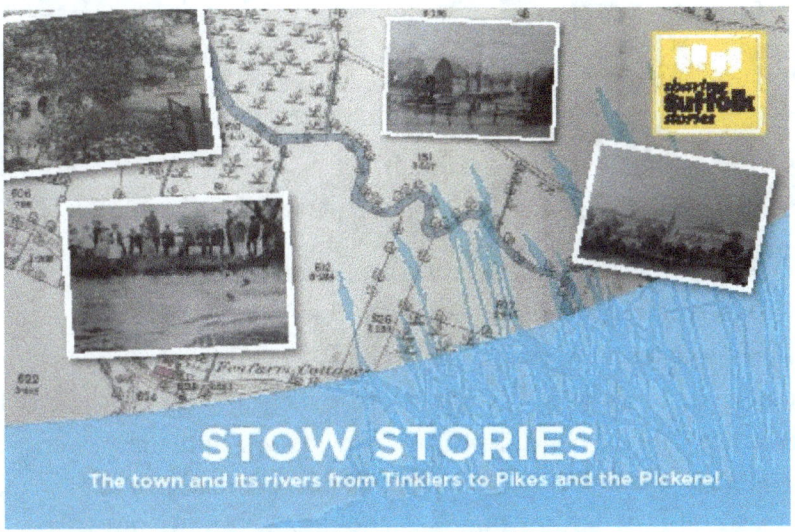

The Rattlesden River Valley Network:

Judith Thompson initiated this network – at the same time as Stow Stories – to connect and involve neighbourhoods, individuals and local organisations with a shared passion for nature on their doorstep, a willingness to 'act for nature,' and a desire for an inclusive society. Brought together by their shared ambition – to raise awareness and encourage action around the biodiversity and climate change crisis – a wide range of groups now support each other's activities and events.

Both Stow Stories and The Rattlesden River Valley Network feed up-to-date project information into the Stowmarket Town Council's Environment Forum and newsletters: www.stowmarkettowncouncil.gov.uk/biodiversity-and-environmental-action/stowmarket-environment-forum

2019 October - Official Stow Stories Launch

Stow Stories was officially launched at The John Peel Centre for Creative Arts in Stowmarket.

www.johnpeelcentre.com

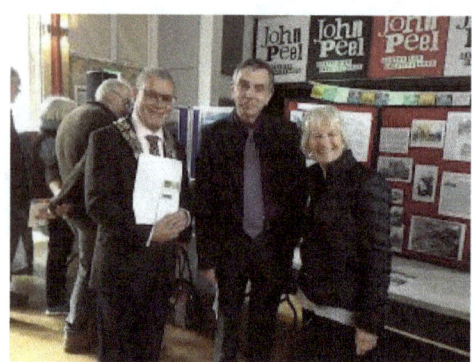 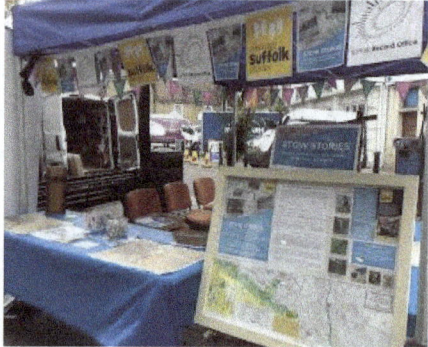

New discoveries by novice researchers:

Judith Thompson, Angela Griggs and Maggie Aldridge (JAM) chose to collaborate in a quest to explore the heritage of the Rattlesden River Valley from Tinkler's Meadow into Stowmarket and the places, people and land, associated with Danecroft Villa as recorded in the Stowmarket Tithe Map (1839), Apportionment Document (1839) and in the deeds of Danecroft Cottage from 1852.

The historic parcel of Danecroft land was JAM's research starting point with a focus on place, people and nature. Through their research they connected to the wider community in and around Stowmarket and the wider world.

A Suffolk Archives Community Learning Officer supported the project. As research gathered pace, information in other Stowmarket historical documents led to new discoveries. Judith Thompson reports: "We used of a broad range of archive resources and consulted widely, for

example with knowledgeable residents and other organisations to explore social history stories including people's occupations, industry and leisure."
– Explore Stowmarket's built and natural heritage
– Uncover Stowmarket's 'sense of place' through time
– Understand how the area's geology, landscape, land qualities and land use influenced town industries and growth
– Chat to people in the community about their memories and record oral histories
– Research the biodiversity of Tinkler's Meadow to Pikes Meadow in Stowmarket
– Connect research to places, people and nature in town and further afield"
Researchers discovered much about the history of Danecroft and Stowmarket.

2021 Stow Story Legacy and Nurture Together Collective

Judith, Angela and Maggie (JAM) agreed that their research should not just look to the past, but also connect with the present day and give a nod to the future. They wanted to maintain Stow Stories as a living history project.

Funding was secured from Suffolk Archives and the National Heritage Lottery for a creative interpretation of Stow Stories. JAM remained open-minded about style and format but agreed at an early stage to carefully respect accessibility and inclusion. The impact of the Covid pandemic also influenced their decisions.

Without a home venue for any creative work, JAM struck upon the idea that residents and visitors could 'take a Stow Stories tour' to discover Stowmarket in a new way. It would be 'more of an interactive quest,' than a trail for people to simply follow.

From the outset there was a strong commitment to involve others and to develop a town wide project. Raising awareness about Stow Stories involved much walking about town to introduce and promote the project to key organisations in order to create interest, involvement and support. In addition to the Nurture Together Collective – which was also founded in 2021 – excellent connections were established with influencers and decision makers Stowmarket Town Council, Suffolk County Council, Mid Suffolk Council, Parish Councils, local churches, environmental groups such as Stowmarket Wildlife Trust. Red Gables Community Hub, Stowmarket Dementia District Community Group, Stowmarket Eco Future Group, local history groups, art centres, the Stowmarket Library, Food Museum.

Nurture Together Collective

Founded in 2021, the Nurture Together Collective's common goal is 'to nurture people, place and nature'. The collective brought together: Stow Stories, Rattlesden River Valley Network, Red Gables, Stowmarket District Dementia Community Group, Get Stowmarket Reading and Stowmarket Eco Future Group. While retaining their separate identities they intended to benefit from working together to reach out and also to involve other organisations.

Over the coming years they would support each other at various events, including Snowdrops for Stowmarket (2021), Christmas Fayres (2021/22), World Earth day (2022) and the Queen Elizabeth II Jubilee celebration at Red Gables (2022) and Primadonna Festivals (2021 onwards).

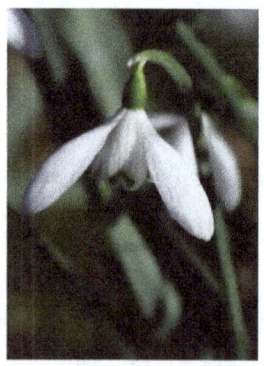 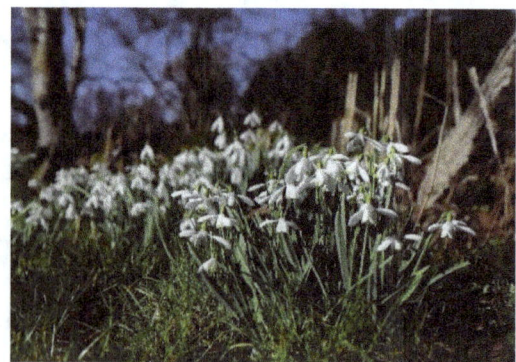

Danecroft snowdrops – photo by Dean Rednall a local nature photographer

2021 to 2023 Stow Stories to Tinkler's Quest

Before making the final decision on how best to share their Stow Stories research in a creative, engaging way with the wider community, JAM explored many options, these included: a festival within a Stowmarket Town Council event, a website, a book, sculpture, film or portable artworks.

While still considering creative options for Stow Stories, Judith was introduced to professional artist Loïs Cordelia who (along with other artists) had been commissioned by Suffolk Libraries to create a mural for a new town project, The Stowmarket Garden Project: 'Stitching Stow,' in Spring 2021.

The 'Stitching Stow' design was heavily rooted in the history of Stowmarket with artworks created throughout the garden inspired by the town. Judith was invited to provide Loïs with an insight into Stowmarket's landscape and biodiversity. Inspired by Judith's information Loïs asked to include Judith's Foreverland poem in her mural, and to name the mural after this poem. Loïs sculpted fifty-one local nature images in her mural.

Following a second collaboration between Loïs and Judith in 2022, when Loïs created a '*Web of Life*' sculpture for the Food Museum in Stowmarket, JAM knew that the multi-talented artist Loïs Cordelia was the perfect fit to create a unique Stow Story creative legacy for the town.

As a first step, JAM invited Loïs to promote the Stow Stories legacy by creating a 'Stowmarket Landmarks' painting. Loïs was commissioned to paint live during a Red Gables event to celebrate the Queen's Platinum Jubilee, to respond artistically to visitor's suggestion about their favourite landmarks' in and around Stowmarket. Funding for this was secured via Nurture Together. The Stowmarket Landmarks' painting would later go on tour at nine venues across the town to raise interest in the forthcoming Tinkler's Quest launch.

'Stowmarket Landmarks' confirmed that Loïs was the right artist for what JAM had in mind. Her artistic and personal skills, along with her empathy for their aspirations, led JAM to offer Loïs the contract to collaborate with them on a far larger Stow Stories legacy project based on JAM's research and knowledge of Stowmarket. It took several months of deliberating artistic styles and town locations before the concept of Tinkler's Quest – a series of storytelling paintings to reflect Stowmarket's past, present and future, and to spark interest across all ages – was defined.

These paintings were to be used in an interactive way, as a community resource to inspire action for nature and to promote Stowmarket's sense of place through time: a place which mattered, a place to be proud of. Another key aim was to establish a new heritage and environment town trail with the message that Stowmarket is a destination and not a passing through place.

Tinkler's Quest:

It was agreed that Tinkler's Quest would be the name of the creative interpretation of Stow Stories research and that painting content would include stories within stories to reflect:
– Research interpretation – places, people, nature
– Images to connect memories and spark conversation
– Layers of interest – landscape, biodiversity, Danecroft, industry
– Elements to represent or symbolise 'bigger' stories
– Intrigue – past, present and future connections
– Essentials - fairy-tale, engaging, magical qualities – with a sense of fun
– Aspects to foster interaction with all age groups
– Reference to industries and Stowmarket raw materials
– Shifts in society through time
– Nature images in Helen Whittaker's stained-glass windows
– Something new for Stowmarket

A Sense of Place:

In selecting the words to include in the Tinkler's Quest paintings and displays, Judith Thompson was inspired by the concept of 'A Sense of Place,' of exploring our connection and belonging to the place, or places, we live.

The paintings evolve:

– Artist and researchers agreed artwork style, size of canvas and numbers

– Judith prepared concept, inspiration and story content for each painting

– Loïs and Judith discussed text and images before Loïs created mock-ups

– Mock-ups were fine-tuned and checked against agreed key principles

– Loïs created final storytelling paintings

Saturday 22 July 2023 – Tinkler's Quest Launch Day

Tinkler's Quest was launched at St Peter's & St Mary's Church with a thanksgiving, celebratory service and a day of family activities which were free and accessible to everyone. The church continued to host the Tinkler's Quest Exhibition for two weeks, after which the eighteen paintings were given to venues across the town.

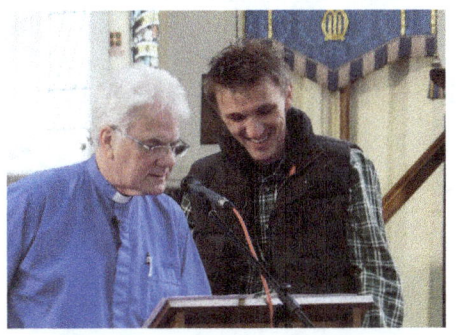
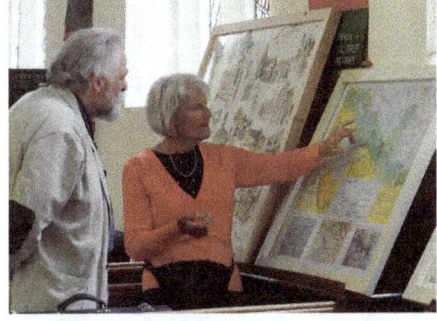
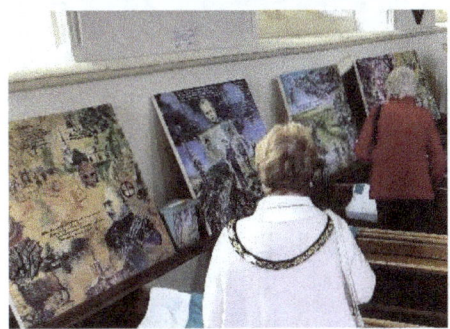
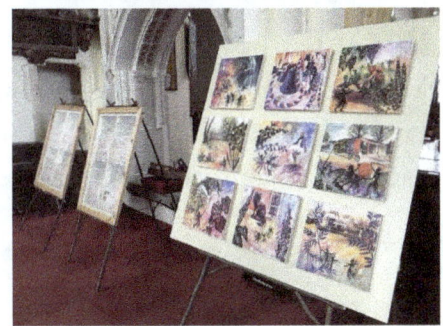

2023 ongoing - Tinkler's Quest – Tinkler's Story Quest Activities

Stow Stories partnered with Get Suffolk Reading to create an interactive Tinkler's Quest Trail for all ages based on the Storytelling paintings. This was launched shortly after the exhibition for the summer of 2023.

2024 ongoing - Tinkler's Quest – Tinkler's Story Quest Activities

Ideas for the Stow Stories – Tinkler's Quest Digital Project were developed with support of key organisations. Funding was secured from Stowmarket Town Council to create full size copies of the painting collections, along with the purchase of easels. These will be used at town events to highlight the natural environment and aspects of the towns heritage to widen access and interest in the project.

Additional funding was secured to ensure painting collections would be as accessible and inclusive as possible, and future-expand Tinkler's Quest activities.

We acknowledge and appreciate the support, involvement and funding for this project from Suffolk County Council - Councillor Keith Welham, Stowmarket Town Council and Nurture Together Collective.

2025 ongoing – Stow Stories - Tinkler's Quest digital - live in 2025:

Stow Stories - Tinkler's Quest digital project is set to be unveiled in 2025, which will offer creative and learning resources across the community to promote conservation – and importantly, to get people talking about, and caring for the place where they live. Tinkler's Quest aims to reach out through the ART of conversation.

2025 What next

Stow Stories – Tinkler's Quest storytelling journey will continue to promote new stories, ideas and resources which nurture the wellbeing of place, people and nature across river, land, sea and sand.

The love of nature – it's beauty, wildness, healing power and loss inspire me to share Stow Stories and Tinkler's Quests knowing that through small or large steps of community action we can all help make the world on our doorsteps wilder again.

Stow Stories -Tinkler's Quest webpage - redgables.org.uk/stow-stories-tinklers-quest

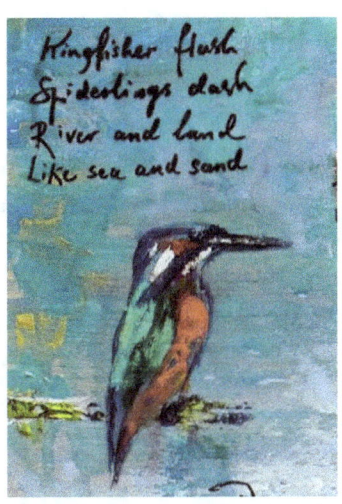

All proceeds from Stow Stories – Tinkler's Quest art trail initiates are donated to Nurture Together Collective

Nurture Together is a collective formed on 31 March 2021 to inspire others to support Stowmarket to become a greener town, encourage people to connect to green spaces to benefit their wellbeing and to protect, restore and enhance the natural world on our doorstep.

Nurture Together based at Red Gables includes, Stow Stories, Rattlesden River Valley Network, Stowmarket and District Dementia Community Group, Stowmarket Eco Future Group and Red Gables.

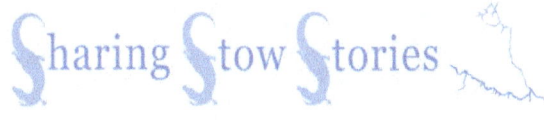

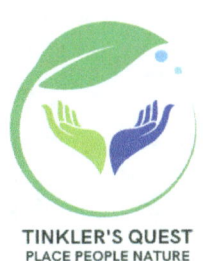

TINKLER'S QUEST
PLACE PEOPLE NATURE

APPENDIX

Links

Explore and discover local action in Stowmarket - an invitation to join in

Tinkler's Quest Art Trail video www.youtu.be/R7xYhYoDd08

Tinkler's Quest – A Journey through Magical Storytelling Paintings e-book

Stowmarket Town Council – find out about Stowmarket a vibrant mid Suffolk town.
www.stowmarkettowncouncil.gov.uk
www.stowmarkettowncouncil.gov.uk/your-town
www.stowmarkettowncouncil.gov.uk/community-groups

Red Gables Wellbeing Hub – Is a lively and inviting community hub in the centre of Stowmarket with spaces accessible for the diverse needs of the local community.
www.redgables.org.uk

Stowmarket & District Dementia Community Group is a volunteer group working towards making Stowmarket and surrounding villages Dementia Friendly. www.redgables.org.uk/sddg

Stowmarket Wildlife Group - wildlife talks / guided walks are held during the year, infolink.suffolk.gov.uk/kb5/suffolk/infolink/service.page?id=CnkIutiwoG8

Eco Future Group - Our group aims to give information and ideas about caring for the environment, living sustainably, and to create opportunities for action.
www.stowmarketecofuturegroup.co.uk

Pickerel Project - The Pickerel Project is a voluntary group seeking to regenerate the River Gipping in Stowmarket and make it nicer for everyone in the town.
www.stowmarkettowncouncil.gov.uk/local-services/pickerel-project

Stowmarket Local History Group - We meet once a month in Stowmarket to talk and share its history. This channel will allow us to bring more of our history to life through videos.
www.youtube.com/@stowmarketlocalhistorygrou7692

Stowupland Local History Group - We share research about the lives of people who used to live or were connected to Stowupland, or the wider Suffolk ...
www.stowuplandlocalhistorygroup.org

The Hold - 900 years of Suffolk's history captured through thousands of documents.
www.suffolkarchives.co.uk
www.suffolkarchives.co.uk/whats-on

The East Suffolk Catchment Partnership newsletters
us3.campaign-archive

Walks and Wanders - *video walks with Don Egan*
walksandwanders.com

Walks and Wanders - Danecroft Diaries
www.youtube.com/@Walksandwanders
Through the year at Danecroft – a hidden cottage and its land, in Stowmarket Suffolk. The following videos are part of a special Walks and Wanders series, filmed in collaboration with Steve and Judith Thompson, the owners of Danecroft, who manage their land in a way that provides habitat for wildlife.

Episode 1: The Hidden Gem
Judith introduces the land and shares stories of snakes, otters and owls.

Episode 2: The Journey
Steve builds a Shepherds Hut and Judith explains the Stow Stories project.

Episode 3 - Tales of the Riverbank - The Woodland and flood
In this episode, I visit Steve and Judith after heavy rainfall caused The River Rat to burst its banks, flooding across their property. We also go for a walk around the other half of their land, a mixture of fen, woodland and bog. We find evidence of badgers, and see where they spotted otters and water voles in previous years. Join us on this secret Stowmarket Walk in a private woodland.

Episode 4 - "Stack the brash" Basket making history Stowmarket
Another visit to Danecroft Cottage in Stowmarket. Looking at the history of basket making in Suffolk, and the osier beds that supplied the willow stems for the local basket-making industry. Some thoughts from Steve's Dad, aged 93. And a beautiful poem from one of Danecroft's past visitors.

Episode 5: Badgers, Boxes and Blooms
Wildlife camera reveals the nightlife, installing owl and bird boxes, and the snowdrops appear.

Episode 6: Stowmarket Springwatch!
Move over Chris Packham! Stowmarket has its own Springwatch team!

Episode 7: A trip down memory lane!
Judith and Steve welcome a couple of special visitors who share their childhood memories of Danecroft and the surrounding area.

Episode 8: Beating the Bounds
Judith and Don go on a short history walk of the area around Danecroft.

Episode 9 : 2,021 snowdrops for 2021!
Judith and Steve donate 2,021 snowdrop bulbs to the town of Stowmarket.

Episode 10: Ecology Students visit Danecroft
Students from Suffolk University examine the River Rat at Danecroft.

www.ingramcontent.com/pod-product-compliance
Lightning Source LLC
Chambersburg PA
CBHW070429290526
45791CB00005B/1903